SPIRITUAL HEALTH

The Key to Mental Health

by
Rosa-Lee Tuffney

Fig.1

GETHSEMANE
Cover image from a painting by Rosa-Lee Tuffney

Print available from
www.rosaleetuffney.com

WELCOME

TO THE WORLD OF SPIRITUAL HEALTH

Fig.2

ROSA-LEE TUFFNEY

DISCLAIMER

This book offers help to those struggling with mental illness. If you are on prescribed medication for a mental health condition, continue taking it. Prescribed medication will not hinder the healing of your spirit.

Prescription drugs treat the body whereas we treat the spirit. Neither treatments conflict. You may wish to advise your doctor about restoring your spirit for then they too will see your recovery.

ISBN: 9798838235206
Copyright © 2022 by Rosa-Lee Tuffney. All rights reserved
Cover Image by Rosa-Lee Tuffney
Contact: rosa@rosaleetuffney.com

CONTENTS

CONTENTS

CONTENTS

CONTENTS

CHAPTER 8. ART TO CALM THE MIND

NOTES

NOTES

CHAPTER 1
TAKING BACK CONTROL

SPIRITUAL HEALTH
THE KEY TO MENTAL HEALTH

I help people overcome mental illness, without toxic medication or GP appointments. Avoiding toxic medication avoids harmful side effects. There are no medical appointments, no prescriptions or waiting lists to see a consultant. If you are looking to cure a mental illness, I can help.

Humankind has forgotten it can self-heal through the spirit. The purpose of this book is to remind us that we can. Using spiritual health to overcome mental illness is what separates this book from all the others on mental health?

Doctors treat mental illness through the body. I treat mental illness through the spirit. Using the spirit is more effective because mental illness is in the spirit, not the body. Mental illness being a disease of spirit means it is the spirit that needs to be healed. Medicating the body will not heal the spirit.

Treating an illness is not the same as curing it. Drugs heal the flesh. They do not heal the spirit because drugs do not reach the spirit. Anti-depressants do not cure depression because they cannot reach to where the depression is. Their name is purposefully disarming for who would take a drug called,

'I don't know what this does, but let's try it anyway?

At best, anti-depressants manage symptoms of depression, though their effect on the body is still a mystery to medical science.

Spiritual health is the key to overcoming mental illness because the illness is in our thoughts and beliefs, which is spirit, not in our arms or our legs.

Thoughts and beliefs have energy but no mass, nor molecules. Nor does mental illness. They are not physical but exist in spiritual form. The energy within thoughts and beliefs come from the spirit, not the beating heart.

Medical science has no language to understand the human spirit, so has no understanding of the health of the spirit or what our thoughts and beliefs are made of.

On the 20th of July 2022, Sarah Knapton, science editor for the Daily Telegraph revealed how scientists at University College London struggle to define mental illness, or what it is made of. They have little idea what chemically formulated antidepressants do to the body. This is a concern as antidepressants are prescribed to one in six adults in England.

Fig. 3

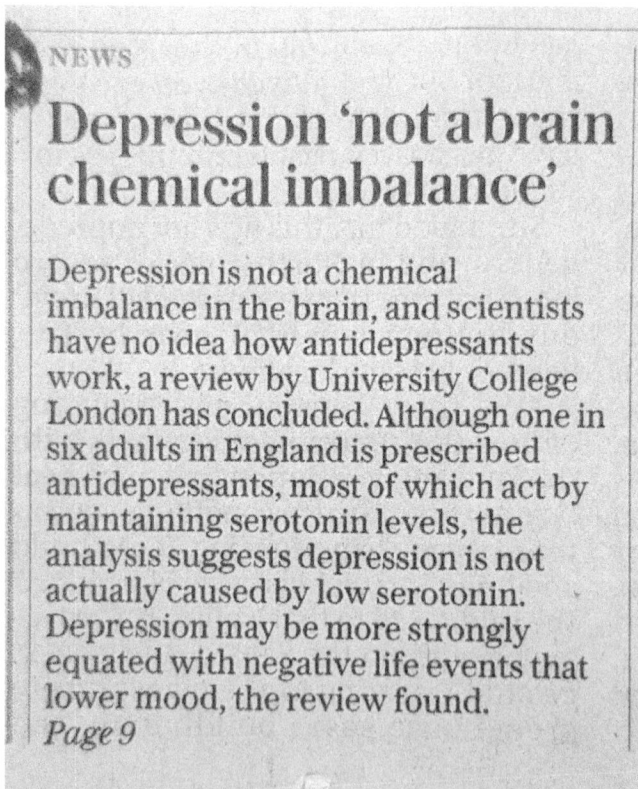

NEWS

Depression 'not a brain chemical imbalance'

Depression is not a chemical imbalance in the brain, and scientists have no idea how antidepressants work, a review by University College London has concluded. Although one in six adults in England is prescribed antidepressants, most of which act by maintaining serotonin levels, the analysis suggests depression is not actually caused by low serotonin. Depression may be more strongly equated with negative life events that lower mood, the review found.
Page 9

CUTTING FROM FRONT PAGE OF THE
DAILY TELEGRAPH 20TH OF JULY 2022

Mental illness such as depression or self-harming stems from negative energy. Until medical science finds a way to recognise the human spirit, and the laws that govern it, mental illness, will remain, to them, a complete mystery. Mental illness will be incurable whatever medication they prescribe.

The brain of someone suffering from a mental illness such as depression or self-harming is no different in structure, quality or appearance than the brain of someone who is perfectly healthy. There is nothing physically different between the two brains because mental illness is not in the flesh of the brain but in the thoughts and beliefs that flow through it.

Because thoughts and beliefs that flow through it are not physical, they leave no physical impairment. The dilemma for mental health experts is, if there is no physical impairment to the brain, what is there to treat?

They must be seen to do something but how do they treat a perfectly healthy brain for a condition that does not exist physically in the brain but in the spiritual energy that flows within it?

We are body, mind and spirit. We are subject to spiritual forces every day. Mental illness feeds off negative spiritual energy. Healing feeds off positive spiritual energy. Spiritual energy is regulated by our thoughts and beliefs. We can regulate the quality of our lives by managing the quality of our thoughts and beliefs. This is made possible by spiritual health.

We are spiritual beings living in physical bodies. We are physical and spiritual. There are effective treatments for healing the physical body as there are effective treatments for healing the spirit.

The body gets a great deal of attention whereas the spirit has been sorely overlooked. There is no sense medicating the body for a condition in the spirit or treating the spirit for a condition in the body. Flesh heals flesh as spirit heals spirit.

Medicating a spiritual illness leads to chronic, persistent, recurrent, or incurable outcomes because the medication does not reach the illness. Mental illnesses are spiritually rooted which means when they are treated medically, rather than spiritually, they often become chronic, persistent, recurrent or incurable.

Until mental illness is redefined as a condition of the spirit, mental illness will remain chronic, persistent, recurrent or incurable no matter what medication mental health experts prescribe.

If mental illness has no molecules or mass, how do we know what it is made of? We know mental illness is made of negative spiritual energy because it impairs the spirit.

A healthy spirit bears fruit. We see this fruit as kindness, patience, empathy, gratefulness, contentment, courage, intuition, foresight, imagination and creativity. These are just a few of the many fruits of the spirit.

Fruits of the spirit disappear during mental illness. Mental illness is the opposite of spiritual fruit. Spiritual fruit comes from positive energy which means mental illness must therefore be negative energy in the spirit. If this were not so, then the fruits of the spirit would not disappear during mental illness.

Negative energy produces fears, phobias, and irrational beliefs. Jealousy, anger, sadness, frustration, self-loathing, guilt, shame and more besides are all rooted in negative energy. They are all symptoms of a spirit in poor health.

Medical science ignores the human spirit because spiritual energy falls outside the laws of science. Without the laws of chemistry, physics and biology medical science has no language with which to even acknowledge the human spirit because it is neither chemical, physical nor biological, but spiritual.

Mental illnesses also fall outside the laws of chemistry, physics and biology but within the laws of spiritual science. Mental health experts have no understanding of spiritual science, nor its laws, therefore no understanding of mental illness. If this were not so, they would be able to cure mental illness and they can't, whereas the laws of spiritual science can.

It is by spiritual laws the human spirit can self-heal. We all have a spirit subject to the same spiritual laws which means we can all self-heal. Somehow, we have forgotten we even have a spirit let alone the laws that enable us to self-heal. These are the laws I am reviving so we can once again self-heal.

Who today thinks for a moment about their spirit? Who even knows what their spirit is, what it does or whether it is even in good health? It is time to recognise our spiritual-self and remind ourselves just how powerful our spirit is. Our spiritual-self is far more amazing than we realise.

A spirit in poor health will impair our quality of life. If we understood how dependent our fortunes in life are on the spirit, it would get a lot more attention than it does. Mental illness, chronic sickness, poverty and misfortune are all symptomatic of a spirit in poor health. All are curable and avoidable with a strong healthy spirit.

Spiritual forces effect every area of our life because our spirit is the essence of who we are. We do nothing without the spirit being involved therefore every area of our life is adversely affected by a neglected spirit in poor health.

Manipulating spiritual laws to our advantage is called spiritual warfare. We can overcome negative spiritual forces adversely affecting our life by weaponizing positive spiritual forces. This is how we can improve life. It is a battle; we have an enemy which is why it is called spiritual warfare.

This book teaches spiritual warfare. The first principle is to know your enemy. Our enemy lies in the forces that hide behind mental illness. It is spiritual in form which means it is subject to the same spiritual laws as we are. We need to know what those laws are if we are to use them against the enemy. We shall learn about spiritual laws later.

Flesh heals flesh as spirit heals spirit but how can we know the difference? Illnesses rooted in the body are successfully treated and healed by medication. Flesh heals flesh because the illness is rooted in the flesh and that is where the medication is applied.

Illnesses rooted in the spirit, such as self-harming, an eating disorder or anxiety, are not successfully healed through medicating the body because it is the wrong treatment being applied to the wrong place. This is why spiritual illnesses often become incurable, chronic, recurrent or persistent.

Certain diseases in the spirit like anxiety or depression cause physical symptoms that can be mistaken for illnesses of the body. Anxiety for instance can cause skin rashes, headaches, tummy pains, dizziness, blurred vision, high blood pressure, and tiredness. These symptoms though in the body are not of the body but of the spirit. Only when the anxiety is treated through the spirit, will the symptoms in the body go.

Mental illness is in the mind. The subconscious mind is connected to the spirit. Spiritual warfare happens in the mind and the spirit, not the body. The mind and spirit become a war zone. With spiritual warfare the body is irrelevant.

Spiritual warfare enables us to retake control of our thoughts and beliefs. Thoughts and beliefs during mental illness are not under our control. They belong to the enemy, which are negative spiritual forces behind mental illness.

All thoughts and beliefs have spiritual energy which is either positive or negative, or in spiritual terms, lawful or lawless. The laws of spiritual science define what is lawful and what is not.

Positive thoughts heal, negative thoughts bring sickness. The placebo effect is a well-documented phenomena proving the power of positive thought. It is even accounted for mathematically by pharmaceutical companies in their drug trials because the placebo effect is predictable and measurable!

Mainstream science accepts the placebo effect as a self-healing ability of the spirit for it is mathematically accounted for in pharmaceutical drug trials but ignores the self-healing ability of the spirit when treating mental illnesses. Therein lays the hypocrisy of mainstream science regarding the human spirit

The healing power of the spirit is widely forgotten. This book will reminds us of this self-healing ability we all have. Our spiritual self is far more amazing than most can imagine.

Self-healing means we can take back responsibility for our health. Today most turn in every instance to the NHS because we have lost confidence to make decisions about our health. Now the NHS is buckling under the weight of a dependent population, created out of its own ambitions.

The medical profession is well known for ignoring or even ridiculing the views of the patient which is why the patient has now lost all confidence in their own judgements regarding health. It is time to change this.

Being unnecessarily dependent on others is not good. It is time to take back responsibility of our health, especially spiritual health, because no one else will be more invested in our health and well-being than we are.

A healthy spirit can self-diagnose, and self-heal. There is much we can do for ourselves but have forgotten how. I want to restore this oversight. We only have one body, mind and spirit and if they break, we don't have a spare. Let's take responsibility for ourselves and start living long healthy lives.

DISCOVERING
THE HUMAN SPIRIT

Who today considers their spirit? This is an extraordinary oversight considering that without it, we do not even exist. Our spirit is the life force within us. It is the only part of us that continues to exist after the body has died and returned to dust. It is the most amazing part of us, with supernatural abilities, and yet we know nothing about it, or even what it does.

We have supernatural abilities, or fruits of the spirit, that guide us through life. These fruits include intuition, foresight, empathy, confidence, insight, courage, patience, kindness, imagination, creativity and many more besides. All these abilities make life easier to navigate and keeps us away from trouble. Life is better with them than without them.

The human spirit is the essence of who we are. In it lies our talents, skills, character, purpose and direction in life. When the spirit is healthy we are the best version of us we can be. A neglected spirit in poor health is smothered by negative energy and produces no fruit to help us thrive. We fall short of all we could be.

A neglected spirit has no immunity from diseases any more than a neglected body has immunity. Poor health impairs immunity whether it is physical or spiritual.

The human spirit comes from the spiritual realm. The spiritual realm is regulated by spiritual laws in the same way earth is regulated by the laws of physics, biology and chemistry. Spiritual science is the study of spiritual laws.

Laws, whether worldly or spiritual, are definitive. They do not evolve or change but were set before creation for they are what creation is hung on and held together by.

The laws of gravity did not evolve over millions of years for if that were the case, things would have floated off the earth and into outer space.

23

Laws are built into creation from the beginning. This means that if the physical realm and spiritual realm were created, they must have had a Creator.

You may well ask, what has a Creator got to do with spiritual health? The answer is, where do you think our spirit came from? Our spirit was created. It has a Creator. Our spirit exists so it must have come from somewhere and been made somehow out of something, by someone. If the spirit is not working properly and needs to be repaired, does it not make sense to go back to the manufacturer?

The maker of our spirit knows what it is made of, and how it is put together because He was the one who assembled it in the first place. If our spirit needs repair, who better to turn to for help? He can either fix it or show us how to fix it ourselves. He has the codes to all creation so repairing a human spirit is not exactly a problem.

The human spirit comes from the spiritual realm. Our spirit is the life force within us which means spiritual energy has life. If spiritual energy has life and comes from the spiritual realm, then there must be life in the spiritual realm. An example of life in the spiritual realm is in the existence of angelic beings.

There are Seraphim, Cherubim, Archangels, angels, fallen angels, and spirits of the Nephilim who are demons. There are spiritual entities, life forms in the spiritual realm. There is life in the spiritual realm, for if this were not so, how is it our spirit is the force of life within us?

To deny the existence of life in the spiritual realm is to deny there is life in our spirit. We know there is life in our spirit for when the spirit leaves our body, we become very dead!

Science tells us there are no such things as angels or demons in the spiritual realm. Logic tells us there are. Angelic beings bear little resemblance in reality to the creations of Hollywood, fine-art, literature or religion. They are immensely powerful beings that manage creation, its vast forces and many moving parts.

Demons are also nothing like modern depictions but operate quietly in the shadows, unseen and devious. They are the forces behind mental illness, self-harming, suicide, jealousy, obsessions, compulsions, addictions and murder. You will see the proof of these unseen forces as we venture into the spiritual realm.

.

Be assured, planet earth is not ending any day soon, nor is it heading to hell in a hand cart. Planet earth is meticulously managed by millions of angelic beings overseen by a highly attentive Creator, who is very proud and possessive of His creation.

Our dimension was made through the spiritual realm, not the other way around. The spiritual realm has more dimensions than our earthly realm so in that sense is more real than our own. How do we know this?

The Creator has painstakingly documented His relationship with us. He has interacted closely with humankind for thousands of years. It has all been recorded in the Dead Sea Scrolls. We are His greatest creation, and He wants us to know it. He has plans for us which He also wants us to know. He would not leave His precious creation unattended, nor would He leave it to humankind to manage.

He asked us to look after the plants and the animals and we have trashed it. Is it any wonder He will not let us near the codes to creation or near the codes to life? To believe we are in charge, responsible or even capable of running creation is laughable.

He knows how flawed and corrupt we are for He made us. If the Creator was genius enough to make creation, do you really think, having made humans, He would leave us in charge? I think not, for what could possibly go wrong I hear you cry. I will prove planet earth is managed by angelic beings from the spiritual realm.

If the human spirit comes from the spiritual realm, how does it get here? The human spirit enters this realm through conception. The spirit is not created at conception but enters this dimension *'through'* conception.

Conception is understood in terms of physics, chemistry and biology. These are the observable elements to conception. What is not observable is the spiritual aspect.

The spirit of life that completes conception is not physical, chemical, or biological so is ignored by medical science. The spirit cannot be created from a chemical or biological process. This means that conception which is chemical and biological may create the conditions for a human spirit to cross from one dimension to another but does not create the human spirit itself. A human spirit cannot be created by any of the elements found on earth for it is spirit.

According to science, life emerged from a primordial soup somewhere on earth, millions of years ago. There are no chemicals on earth, however combined, that can create a soup from which life can emerge. No chemicals on earth however arranged can create a single living spirit, whether human, animal, angelic or demonic. No chemicals on earth, however they may be combined, can create any form of life, period!

All living spirits were created by the Creator in the spiritual realm. Those who reject this truth struggle to explain how the human spirit is able to create itself out of nothing, from nowhere and miraculously turn up at conception. Nor can they explain what happens to the spirit, or where it goes when we die?

All these mysteries are revealed in The Dead Sea Scrolls. It is from these scrolls that the Torah and the Bible originated but do not think for a minute the scrolls have anything to do with religion. They don't. They warn us to stay away from religion for they have everything to do with spiritual health, the Creator of the spirit and the meaning of life.

The religions that came from the Torah and the Bible have nothing to do with the Creator of our spirit or spiritual health or the Dead Sea Scrolls. Religion is something else that I explain later. The scrolls warn us against these religions.

If the Dead Sea Scrolls are a record of the relationship between the Creator in the heavenly realm and humankind, how come we don't know about them? They have been hidden because they undermine mainstream science, academia and religion.

The scrolls reveal the origins of life, creation, and the age of the planet, spiritual health, what will happen at the end of this age, and the age to come. All these things directly contradict mainstream science and academia.

The scrolls reveal the purpose of humankind, the meaning of life, the mystery of death and the keys to eternal life, which directly contradicts religion.

They reveal the threats to our health that exist in the spiritual realm, angelic and demonic life forms, the importance of spiritual health, and how to overcome mental illness, which directly contradicts medical science.

It is no wonder that what is written in the Dead Sea Scrolls is kept under wraps for they contradict just about everything we have been told is true. I am going to reveal what it in the Dead Sea Scrolls so you can see for yourself. We are going to test what they say so you can see first-hand they are 100% credible. You will be amazed.

Neither science, academia nor religion have bothered to test the scrolls themselves for if they did they would not be so keen to mock them. Professor Albert Einstein once said, condemnation before an investigation is the height of ignorance. I agree! Sadly, mainstream science, academia and religion don't.

The quality of our thoughts and beliefs enable us to interact with the world around us far more skilfully. When we treat the world around us well, so the world around us treats us well. When we don't, then nor does the world around us. As the adage goes,

What we think about, we bring about.

The quality of our thoughts and beliefs regulate positive and negative energy. When we know the laws of the spirit we can direct spiritual energy to enhance our quality of life. In short, we can thrive.

No matter how hopeless our situation, we can restore our spirit so it bears fruit and by learning the spiritual laws of life, we can thrive. The odds of success without the fruits of the spirit are stacked against us. A healthy spirit produces a lot of fruit, stacking the odds of success in our favour. Let's go and grow some spiritual fruit.

DIAGNOSING A SPIRIT
IN POOR HEALTH

How do we diagnose the health of our spirit? How can something that does not physically exist even have health issues? Spiritual health is dependent on the quality of spiritual energy within it. A neglected spirit is smothered by negative energy, whereas a healthy spirit radiates positive energy.

The health of the spirit can be seen by our nature. A soul whose nature is selfish, unkind, impatient, angry, cowardly, lazy, immoral, violent, controlling, dishonest, unfaithful, ungrateful and needy has a spirit in poor health. These are all character traits of a spirit in poor condition.

They are traits of a carnal nature. A carnal nature is the opposite of a spiritual nature and thrives when the spirit is in poor health. The carnal-self is the opposite of our spiritual-self.

The health of the spirit can also be diagnosed by our quality of life. Mental health problems, chronic, persistent or recurrent physical health problems, poverty, misfortune, lack of opportunity, lack of confidence, low self-esteem, and an inability to communicate with others, infertility, toxic relationships, and divorce, are all symptoms of a neglected spirit in poor health.

It is plain to see by a person's nature, health and quality of life how healthy their spirit is. How different a life is when the spirit is healthy and bearing lots of fruit. It is easy to diagnose the health of the spirit of many of those around us even if they have no concept of these things themselves.

A healthy spirit brings abundance, loving stable relationships and a joyous life. A healthy spirit raises the quality of life as a neglected spirit lowers it. Good fortune favours the spiritually healthy year after year. This is the whole point to restoring the health of the spirit. We can clearly see those with healthy spirits.

Many people blame their misfortune on the world around them or on others. Blame seldom improves anything. Rooting out the cause does. The most common cause of misfortune is a neglected spirit because it will bring misfortune upon itself. Until the spirit is healed life will not improve because the poor soul will continue to make the same mistakes over and over.

Many souls endure years of unnecessary struggle because their carnal nature, stemming from a neglected spirit, impairs their ability to interact successfully with the world around them.

They invite upon themselves misfortune quite unknowingly. Their fortunes would be transformed if only their spirit bore some fruit such as intuition, foresight, insight, empathy, intuition, imagination, and creativity.

Fruits that come from a healthy spirit enable us to make better life choices. We know who we are, why we are here and where we are going. We are self-assured because we know our destiny, our talents, skills and the contribution in life we are born to make. We have purpose and direction. We have something to aim for and a reason for doing it.

Our spiritual self is the highest version of ourselves we can be. We have countless supernatural abilities ensuring our success. Our adventure into the spiritual realm starts here. It is time to meet our spiritual-self.

WHERE DOES
MENTAL ILLNESS COME FROM?

Mental illness is not physical. We cannot see it, touch it or smell it, so where is it and even more interestingly, where does it come from? We know it is somewhere in our thoughts and beliefs which we also cannot see, touch or smell. As enemies go, mental illness is one of the stealthiest enemies we can have. That does not mean we cannot overcome it, because we can!

Mental illness is a disease of the spirit. Diseases are spread by pathogens. Pathogens are organisms that bring disease. Spiritual pathogens bring disease to the spirit. Spiritual diseases present as mental illness, chronic sickness, misfortune and poverty.

A neglected spirit in poor health has no immunity to spiritual pathogens and is vulnerable to spiritual attack just as a neglected body in poor health has no immunity from biological pathogens and is vulnerable to biological attack.

Pathogens, spiritual or biological bring disease, one to the spirit and the other to the body. Immunity is dependent on health whether it is physical or spiritual.

Healing the spirit restores immunity. Mental illness comes from spiritual pathogens. We will consider the origin and nature of spiritual pathogens later. The truth is fascinating.

PLEASE NOTE:
For those dependent on prescribed medication, please don't stop taking it! Your medication will not hinder the healing of your spirit. Self-healing through the spirit will not affect any prescribed medication, nor will that medication prevent us healing the spirit.

Self-healing through the spirit has no harmful side effects whatsoever. We encourage you to work with your GP for he too will then see that very soon you will no longer need prescribed medication. Let's all work together.

HOW DO I FIGHT
AN INVISIBLE ENEMY?

Mental illness is invisible but don't let that discourage you. We have strategies to expose this invisible enemy. An invisible enemy gives us two challenges. The first is where is it? The second is how do we fight it?

Let us consider first the question of, where is it? We know the enemy lurks behind mental illness. It is not physical which is why we cannot see it and why it does not respond to medication. This invisible enemy is in our thoughts and beliefs, so we know where it is. The war zone to retake control of our thoughts and beliefs is in our mind.

Spiritual warfare enables us to retake control of our thoughts and beliefs. Our power lies in what we think and believe. Changing our thoughts and beliefs means we can weaponizing them against the enemy. This is how we regain control of our mind. We have a powerful strategy for doing this.

The spiritual pathogens behind mental illness thrive on negative thoughts and beliefs. They cannot tolerate positive thoughts and beliefs. The battle is lost or won on the quality and strength of our positive thoughts and beliefs as we use them as weapons against mental illness.

If negative beliefs are stronger than positive beliefs, mental illness thrives, if positive beliefs are stronger than negative beliefs, mental illness dies. Spiritual warfare is fought on the quality and strength of thoughts and beliefs. In our own strength it is very hard. When we harness the spiritual power of the Creator, we have all the power we need to heal ourselves.

Negative forces are always harmful and destructive. They do not come from within us. They do not belong to us. They are the enemy behind mental illness. They come from the spiritual realm. They attack us like a biological disease attacks a body.

How do we know spiritual pathogens behind mental illness don't come from within us but from the spiritual realm? We know this because if they came from within us and were of us, we would have control over them. We don't, so they must come from elsewhere. If these negative spiritual forces come from somewhere else, how do we let them in? I will show you how easy it is to let spiritual pathogens in without even realizing it.

The definition of mental illness is loss of control over our thoughts and beliefs. But who or what have we lost control to? Control over our thoughts and beliefs is lost during mental illness to an unseen enemy from the spiritual realm that seeks to cause us harm.

The enemy's thoughts are always negative, malevolent and harmful. Ours aren't. This is how we discern the difference. We can locate this unseen spiritual enemy by separating our thoughts and beliefs from its. We can discern our thoughts for they are not self-destructive and we have control over them. This is how we can separate them from the enemy.

Someone suffering anxiety can recognise anxious thoughts from the enemy. They are the thoughts they don't want but can't stop. They are thoughts over which they have no control, which means they must belong to the enemy. With discernment we can recognise them for what they are and separate ourselves from them.

A thought may be in our head, but that does not make it ours. Spiritual pathogens can put thoughts into our head that we think are ours but are not. The Creator can also put thoughts into our head that are not ours. They are called revelations.

Suicidal thoughts may be in our head but are never ours. The Creator never gave us a nature to destroy ourselves. He is the giver and the taker of life. All life belongs to Him. It was never His intention to give us life and then the mental capacity for us to take it.

So where do such thoughts come from? They come from the powers of darkness in the spiritual realm. They are not ours because He never gave us a mind to take our own life so such a mind must come from elsewhere.

Self-destruction is not part of our spiritual nature, or the spiritual nature of any living creature. We do not see animals in the wild committing suicide. The nature of the spirit is never self-destructive for it goes against the spiritual laws of life.

Mental illness is always negative, dark, malevolent and harmful. It never brings good things, never heals or makes life better. Whoever heard of a mental illness where someone suffers from extreme kindness or generosity? I don't think so!

Spiritual pathogens are always malevolent and destructive. This suggests they know good from evil for they are always evil and never good. To know this is to be sentient. They have intelligence. We are fighting an enemy with intelligence. We shall fight back with intelligence.

We know the enemy is spiritual. We know it is malevolent and evil. We know it is subject to the spiritual laws of life because it is spirit in form. So where do we find the spiritual laws of life? They are in the Dead Sea Scrolls. The laws we need for spiritual protection are found in the ten commandments.

If the spiritual laws of life we need to overcome mental illness are in the ten commandments, how is it we know nothing about them? How is it they are ignored by mainstream science and academia? Why are they so mocked if they have the power for the human spirit to self-heal? They are ignored because they undermine science, the same science that cannot heal the conditions we could heal if we were reminded that we can self-heal.

Without the ten commandments there is no belief, for without knowledge there is no understanding and we cannot believe in something we don't know or understand. Without belief, there is only disbelief. These is no power in disbelief.

Those who believe exclusively with science are left with nothing spiritual in which to believe. They have nothing to feed the spirit for there is no spiritual understanding. Science says the spiritual realm does not exist.

Without understanding there is no spiritual health, empowerment or self-healing. Well done mainstream science!

Disbelief in the spirit realm and its laws prevents self-healing. Disbelief in the Creator prevents us accessing His power needed to self-heal. His spirit needs to indwell ours. That is what gives us the power to self-heal. It is not possible to summon the spiritual power we need to self-heal if we don't believe that spiritual power even exists.

The force of life within us is spiritual which means life is a spiritual force. When it is in the body we are alive. When it leaves the body, we are dead. If the difference between being dead or alive is the spirit then surely the spirit must be life which means it must exist. Mainstream science does not grasp this, because they can't put in in a test tube and measure it.

If we agree the spirit exists, then it must have come from somewhere. But where? The clue is in the word 'spirit'. Is it so difficult to believe the human spirit, which is spirit in energy, spirit in form and subject to spiritual laws, comes from the spiritual realm? If the human spirit comes from the spiritual realm then there must be life in the spiritual realm which means there must have been a Creator. This is completely logical and completely anti-science. I think science is the one with the problem.

The Creator has interacted with humankind from the beginning. It would not make sense if He didn't considering we are His greatest creation. Angelic entities also interact with humankind and have done so from the beginning.

Angelic beings contributed to the writing of the Dead Sea Scrolls. I prove this later. Angelic beings give us an account of creation and how it all came to be. Science mocks it without testing it. It is an account worth testing, so we will test them together in this book, and you will see that the results are astounding.

The Dead Sea Scrolls give us prophecies foretelling the history of earth and humankind in advance. We are meant to know about the spiritual realm for therein lies the meaning and purpose of life on earth, death and the eternal life to come. We need this knowledge if we are to thrive and prosper. Without it life is meaningless, and without purpose or direction. We test the prophecies in the Dead Sea Scrolls for they are scientifically inexplicable. How can anyone know the future in advance? That would suggest intelligent beings in another dimension that is outside time and space. A spiritual realm no less. The prophecies either came true or they did not. We will test them ourselves together in this book. The results will blow your socks off.

Mainstream science and academia mock the Dead Sea Scrolls preferring the theories of evolution by Charles Darwin, published in the 1850s. Darwin was not even a scientist but a theologian. He studied God at Cambridge, graduated, then claimed God doesn't exist. How does that work?

Mainstream science teaches that creation started when something happened, sometime in the past, somewhere, somehow and all the things we see today just evolved out of nothing, from nowhere, by themselves, but there was a big bang! How do we know mainstream science is right? Because Charles Darwin told us back in the 1850s. All sorted!

Why are we questioning creation? What has that got to do with spiritual health? The reason is because our spirits were created on the first day of creation so to dismiss the creation account in the Dead Sea Scrolls is to dismiss the origins of our spirit.

We cannot ignore creation because it relates to the meaning of life and what happens when we die and the eternal life to come. It is all built into creation. Without understanding what happens at the beginning we cannot understand what is happening now or what is to come. We lose our understanding of the spirit for there is no foundation without understanding creation.

Science believes in evolution. Any evidence to the contrary has been hidden or destroyed by mainstream science. Archaeological and skeletal evidence disproving evolution has been destroyed and false evidence presented to support evolution such as the Piltdown man skeleton and the skeleton of 'Lucy' which we cover later. The first is an outright hoax and the second so speculative as to prove nothing.

What do the Dead Sea Scrolls have to do with spiritual health and overcoming mental illness? Two of the scrolls, Enoch and Jubilees, reveal who and what the spiritual entities are behind mental illness. They tell us their origin, and how to overcome them. They show us the art of spiritual warfare.

Spiritual warfare is the art of applying laws that are in the ten commandments to overcome spiritual pathogens. Laws are definitive and predict outcomes whether physical or spiritual.

The law of thermodynamics predicts that touching something hot will burn. Spiritual laws are just as definitive. Knowing what is lawful and what is not means we can apply spiritual laws to predict outcomes in our life. Applying positive laws means we can predict positive outcomes to our life. The ten commandments are those positive laws. They bring positive outcomes.

Spiritual pathogens fear the ten commandments because they generate positive energy which they cannot tolerate. Positive energy destroys them. This is how we can weaponize the commandments for our own protection. This is their power.

The ten commandments keep our thoughts and beliefs in positive territory. They keep us away from fear, anxiety, sadness, depression, hopelessness, anger, jealousy, rejection, shame, guilt and frustration. These are all conditions spiritual pathogens need to survive. Removing them means our soul becomes positive territory that the spiritual pathogens cannot tolerate, so leave or do not enter.

The ten commandments give us power to take back control. So where does this power come from? Keeping the commandments invites the Creator's spirit to dwell within our spirit. There is nothing else on earth that can do this. The commandments are truly unique. They are spiritual laws.

When the Creator's spirit dwells with ours it changes our spiritual DNA. This is where the power comes from to overcome mental illness, to self-heal and to heal others, to break free of chronic sickness, poverty and overcome misfortune.

Our spirit is meant to be connected with the spirit of the Creator, like a smart device going online. How smart is a smart device without the internet? Not that smart! How powerful is a human spirit without the Creator? Not that powerful! When the connection is made, the human spirit becomes supernatural. It is empowered like a smart device going online.

The first law of spiritual warfare is to know your enemy and the second is to know ourselves. Because we are strangers to our own spirit, few of us know who we truly are which means we have some work to do. The knowledge we need, to know we are in the spirit, is in the Dead Sea Scrolls.

We learn what our spirit is and what it can do. It is the most amazing part of us yet sorely overlooked. Most have no idea about their spirit nor its amazing abilities. Because of this, most of us do not really know ourselves. We need to change this if we are going to use spiritual warfare, for the second law requires us to know ourselves.

We need to know how we allowed the spiritual pathogens behind mental illness in to start with. We can't shut the door until we know where the door is.

We leave the door open to them every time we break the commandments. Breaking laws is to be lawless. Lawlessness opens the door to spiritual pathogens. If we don't know what those laws are, then how can we know if we are leaving the door open or not? How can we even know if we are being lawful or not? We need to know the ten commandments for our own spiritual protection and health.

Generations in the UK have no knowledge of the ten commandments, leaving millions of souls unprotected and vulnerable to spiritual pathogens of mental illness, chronic sickness, poverty and misfortune. This is what we see today with one in six people in England are now being prescribed antidepressants.

Dwelling on lawless thoughts brings lawless outcomes, just as touching something hot will burn. Mental illness begins with lawless thoughts and beliefs, which are thoughts and beliefs that break the ten commandments. Who knew?

Dwelling on lawless thoughts generates lawless energy, they grow, and before we know it, they have a life of their own. They are seized by the lawless pathogens whereupon we lose control. The moment we lose control the situation becomes a mental illness. Pathogens seek to control. And that loss of control is the definition a mental illness.

We hear comments like, "I don't know what I was thinking, I was not in my right mind, or that is not like me, or I don't know what made me do it, I was not in control, it was a moment of madness."

We can have thoughts in our head that don't even belong to us. Most believe the thoughts in their head are all theirs. This is not true because some thoughts in our head, do not come from us. They may be in our head but that does not mean that we put them there.

A person contemplating suicide is not putting suicidal thoughts into their own head but are being seduced by evil pathogens leading them to self-destruction. No one in their right mind kills themselves, so whose mind are they in? They are in the mind of the spiritual pathogens I have been speaking about.

How do we know suicide is unnatural? Our spirit is made in the image of the Creator and the Creator is not suicidal or self-destructive. It makes no sense to create life and then give it the capacity to destroy itself.

That goes against the spiritual laws of life which state, do not commit murder, for suicide is murder. Even your own life is not yours to take, for it does not belong to you but to the Creator who gave it to you as a gift.

If suicide was natural or lawful we would see it in nature which we don't for animals in the wild do not commit suicide. The point I am making is that it is possible to have destructive thoughts in our head that are not ours!
We can also have positive thoughts in our head that are not ours. These are revelations, eureka moments of great clarity that popped up as if from nowhere.

Our subconscious mind is connected to our spirit. Our spirit receives and transmits information to and from the spiritual realm continuously, without us realizing it is happening. This information goes through the fruits of the spirit such as intuition, foresight, insight, revelation, imagination and creativity. Our subconscious mind is constantly streaming information from the spiritual realm.

We receive information from the Creator through our subconscious mind. This is how He speaks to us and how we hear Him. Thoughts and beliefs are put into our mind through intuition, revelation and dreams, Our spirit receives and transmits information to and from the spiritual realm all the time, without us even realizing it.

Some of the information is from the heavenly realm and some is from the demonic realm. Being a human spirit, we are connected to both. If we let heavenly forces in our quality of life stays high and life is good, if we let demonic forces in, life becomes a struggle.

CHAPTER 2
WHAT IS THE HUMAN SPIRIT?

WHAT IS
THE HUMAN SPIRIT?

Every living creature on earth has a spirit for it is the force of life within it. Our spirit is the essence of who we are. It is also known as our soul. The soul and spirit cannot be divided as they are the same. The terms spirit and soul are interchangeable.

Before our spirit entered this world through the portal of conception, we were suspended outside time and space in the heavenly realm. We have existed in spirit form from the first day of creation. Man was fashioned from the earth and given life on the sixth day of creation, but the spirits of humankind were all made on the first day.

These things have been made known to humankind by the Angel of the Presence who contributed to the scrolls of Enoch and Jubilees, two of the Dead Sea Scrolls.

We are spiritual beings living in physical bodies. We may lose a limb or one of our waking senses such as hearing or sight and be no less alive; we are no less a person. We are still complete in our spirit even if our body is impaired.

Our spirit inhabits the body, but it is not physically encased because it is not physical in form. It is mysteriously anchored to the first cell of our earthly existence. We know this because it is the spirit that gives the first cell of our existence life. Without the spirit, a single cell of life would not have life.

Every sentient creature has a spirit, is separate and unique from every other spirit that has ever existed. No two spirits are the same, not identical twins nor even conjoined twins. Our spirit is who we truly are. It is the part of us that outlives the body and has the potential to be eternal.

The root of our being is the spirit, not the body which means our true appearance is not that of our body but that of our spirit. The spirit, being invisible means none of us knows what we really look like.

We recognise each other by the shape and size of our bodies, not by our spirit. For some of us older souls whose bodies are past their prime, that can be quite a relief. I am happy to believe that spiritually I am drop-dead gorgeous.

We are physical in body and spirit in energy which means we have a physical carnal self and a spiritual self. So, which bit is which? The part of us that is not spirit is carnal. The part of us that is not carnal is spirit. There is nothing in between.

Our carnal nature craves constant attention and gratification through our waking senses of sight, sound, taste, touch and smell. It needs to be constantly fed, reassured and tended. Our carnal-self is high maintenance.

It is loud, needy and thrives on consumption taking anything it wants, whenever it wants it. Carnality is the opposite of spirituality. We can regulate these two natures within ourselves, allowing either one to become our dominant nature.

The carnal-self does not like being told what to do by anyone, including the spiritual-self or the Creator. It constantly wants its own way and is ever hungry for more delight. It has no concept of restraint or self-discipline.

Spiritual pathogens appeal to our carnal-self because it is easily tempted, seduced, and ever hungry for more, making it gullible and predictable. Eating disorders, substance abuse, self-harming and compulsive behaviour satisfy the desires of the carnal-self.

Carnal lifestyles are indulgent and symptomatic of a neglected spirit in poor health. A weak, neglected spirit cannot control carnal desires. Left unchecked the carnal-self will run amok in its search for evermore gratification.

Our spiritual side is made in the image of the Creator. Our carnal nature is not. Our spiritual nature is rooted in love, our carnal desire is rooted in consumption. Carnal souls seldom know the meaning of love, mistaking it for lust. Lust is a carnal emotion hungry for satisfaction. It does not give as love gives but takes as lust takes. Love is spiritual energy; lust is carnal energy. Sadly, many cannot tell one from the other.

The carnal and the spiritual are in constant conflict. The purpose of the free will is to choose between the carnal and the spiritual self. This choice determines our ultimate destiny and eternal life. No other decision in life has more far-reaching consequences yet none of these things are taught or made known. I will share these things with you.

Our spirit is rooted in love. So, what is love? Love is a spiritual force. It is patient and kind, it does not envy nor boast, it is not proud. It does not dishonour others, it is not self-seeking, it is not easily angered, and keeps no record of wrongs. Love is long suffering. Love is a fruit of the spirit that leads us to become the highest version of ourselves we can be. Love will lead us to eternal life for it is embedded into the ten commandments.

Our spiritual nature is the highest version of ourselves we can be. We live not to consume but to give and to serve. We love others and all that is around us. Our faith is not in ourselves, our money, our fame, our vanity, our power, our possessions and prestige, but in the Creator who empowers our spirit and brings to us everything we need and want to us.

An empowered spirit bears fruit such as confidence, contentment, self-assuredness, courage, generosity, empathy, kindness, gratefulness imagination and creativity. These are attributes of the Creator's nature, whose spirit dwells within them, which is why they reflect His image.

Our carnal nature hates the Creator and seeks lawless energy which is harmful to the spirit. A carnal nature supresses and dominates the spirit. Learning the spiritual laws of life means we can determine lawfulness from lawlessness. Only by this knowledge can we empower the spirit to reign-in the carnal side and its recklessness. For it is written,

'My people perish through lack of knowledge.'

Lack of spiritual knowledge impairs spiritual strength and allows the carnal-self to run amok. When the carnal-self is in the driving seat, it will be a bumpy ride. Ignorance of what is lawful and what is not blinds a soul to the threats around them. They live by fate which seldom ends well.

Laws are definitive and immutable and are not subjective or open to interpretation. What someone may think, feel or choose does not make it law. Spiritual right and wrong is not subjective but defined by laws. Righteousness is spiritually lawful, and sin is spiritually lawless. Righteousness is specific and is found in the ten commandments. Sin is specific for it is to live outside the ten commandments.

When people say, I have my truth and you have your truth, they are speaking nonsense. This is a deceitful corruption of the word, 'truth' mixing it up with the word experience. Truth is defined spiritually by spiritual laws, not by someone's opinion.

We cannot have our own truth for that would mean we are all living under our own separate laws which is nonsense. We are all subject to the same laws, so subject to the same truth. We cannot go around changing the meanings of words or making laws up to suit ourselves.

Spiritual laws have existed from the beginning of time, like gravity, the tides of the seas or the seasons of the year. The laws that hold creation together will not change on the whims of humankind.

The foolish make up their own laws of life with no understanding of what is spiritually lawful or not. They fully believe they are doing right and good but in truth are being lawless. Many Christians fall into this category. I prove this later.

We cannot make up what we think is right and wrong just because we think it is good and kind or that it suits us. Our personal judgement or opinion regarding what is right or wrong is spiritually meaningless. Let me show you.

A person can go to Church on Sunday, donate generously to a Christmas charity, help put up a Christmas tree, and promise to organise an easter egg hunt for the children next easter. These acts appear good and kind but are spiritually lawless according to the spiritual laws of life.

Each of them breaks the ten commandments. I explain how this is so later in the book. The truth is very surprising. The point I am making is what we may think is good, kind and righteous may well be spiritually sinful and lawless according to the spiritual laws of life.

Arguing whether the commandments are fair or not is futile because they are eternal laws, they are immutable. It would be like arguing that when I touch something hot, it is really unfair that I get burnt.

A constant hurdle when explaining spiritual health is people's reluctance to draw toward the Creator for fear that it will lead to a religion.. Firstly, the Creator has nothing to do with religion. He is anti-religion which I prove later.

Religion has done more to put people off the Creator than Satan ever could We need the Creator because He made us. He is the manufacturer of our spirit. He knows how it works and how to repair it. If our car or washing machine breaks down, do we not go back to the manufacturer to have it repaired? Is that being religious? I think not!

Those who try and heal the spirit without their maker risk falling into the occult. Only the Creator is safe territory in the spiritual realm. Anything else in the spiritual realm is negative, satanic, demonic and belongs to the occult. That is why we must connect with the Creator in all matters of the spirit for without His protection we are vulnerable to dark forces.

Spiritual energy is either positive or negative. There is no such thing as neutral energy for that would be neither positive nor negative. Everything in creation is either positive or negative. There is no third option.

The term 'Satan' is not a name but means adversary. It is to oppose as in being the opposite. The opposite of positive, therefore it is negative.

This defines negative spiritual energy is satanic. Therefore, anything that breaks the commandments is not of the Creator, so is by definition, Satanic.

Religion does not keep the Creator's commandments so, by their own scriptures, is satanic. We cover this more later.

Those who try healing the spirit using crystals, herbs and elixirs, tarot cards, horoscopes, hypnotherapy, religion, runes or palmistry, however well meaning, fall outside positive territory, so is satanic. Satanic forces are harmful to spiritual health, so we don't go there.

Satanic realms belong to the occult; The word occult means secret. This is dangerous territory for the spirit, so we avoid it. We need the Creator if we are to restore the health of our spirit and to stay safe. He is the only one we can trust.

SPIRITUAL LAWS

The idea of a free spirit is not as free as we might imagine. The spirit is not free to do what it wants but is regulated by laws of the spirit just as the body is regulated by the laws of physics, chemistry and biology. The earth is regulated by the laws of nature, gravity, the tides, the sun, the moon and the stars. Creation is held together by a myriad of unseen laws. There are earthly laws and there are spiritual laws.

Accepting there is a human spirit is to accept that there are spiritual laws because nothing in creation exists outside laws. Spiritual laws were once taught in every school in the UK, displayed in every courtroom, church and government building for they are in the ten commandments.

Out of the Dead Sea Scrolls came the Bible and in the Bible were the ten commandments. They were hijacked by religion and used as a weapon to beat the nonbeliever into religious submission and obedience. The nonbelievers understandably rejected the ten commandments, believing them to be nothing more than religious doctrine.

They are not, for they were hijacked. Religion may falsely lay claim to them but does not even keep them! Because of the antics of religion most reasonable souls reject the ten commandments as religious guff. I will prove to you that they are anything but religious. They are spiritual laws, not religious doctrine.

Today, many mock the ten commandments despite having no idea what they are, where they are from or what they do. They live in ignorance of the spiritual laws that govern every aspect of their life, for their spirit is the very essence of who they are. Our spirit is in everything we do.

No longer are the ten commandments allowed in the public square, nor in state run schools, nor in courtrooms even though our judicial system was founded opon them, nor in government buildings for many officials consider them offensive.

The truth is the ten commandments are a gift from the Creator for all of humankind for they are spiritual laws that govern our spirit. We all have a spirit that is subject to them which means they are for all of us.

When the Creator gave Moses the commandments, did He say, "Hey Moses, save these commandments for the Christians and the Jews so they can use them to separate themselves from everyone else. No! They are for everyone because we all have a spirit that needs spiritual health.

Breaking laws is to be lawless whether we know we are breaking them or not. There is little hope for a soul to live a lawful life if they have no idea what the law is. This widespread falling away of the law was prophesied two thousand years ago in the scroll of Revelation as a sign of the last days. We can see for ourselves those days are here now!

Keeping the ten commandments does not make someone religious, but the very opposite for they are becoming spiritually empowered, the very thing religion hates. It is not possible to keep the commandments and be faithful to religion at the same time.

Those who keep the commandments don't go to church, attend Sunday services, or wear crosses or crucifixes, nor do they celebrate Easter or Christmas or have their infants baptised, drive around with self-righteous bumper stickers, for these are the doctrines of religion that violate and defy the ten commandments.

Many ask, what about Judaism? That is a religion that keeps the Torah in which the 10 commandments are written, so surely they keep them. Nope! The first commandment asks for belief in the Creator. The Hebrew title for the Creator is Elohim, which is plural. There were two of them, the Father and the Son.

The Jews do not recognise the Son through whom creation was made. They falsely accused Him of blasphemy, had Him flogged and then crucified Him. Not a good start to keeping the commandments. If you can't get past the first one, the rest don't matter.

Keeping the commandments, empowers the spirit. It is the foundation to spiritual health. It is not possible to restore the health of the spirit without the commandments.

The commandments are to the soul what the internet is to a smart-device. The commandments connect our spirit to the Creator. This changes everything for our soul does not go digital but inter-dimensional.

The commandments enable the Creator's spirit to dwell within a human spirit. This empowers the spirit and transforms lives.

Good fortune, good health, joy, peace and abundance are not down to luck or chance but are spiritually lawful outcomes to keeping spiritually positive laws, which are defined by the ten commandments.

Doors open and opportunities appear because positive lawful energy attracts positive lawful outcomes. I will show you how to unlock these forces and you will see for yourself how your life can be transformed.

MAINSTREAM SCIENCE
AND THE SPIRIT

Mainstream science has no mechanism or language to recognise or measure the human spirit. Because science cannot recognise the human spirit it deems it anti-science. This means science cannot understand the spiritual realm or spiritual science or the spiritual laws of life. Nor can they comprehend the true causes of spiritual diseases such as mental illness.

Outright rejection of the spiritual realm has led to widespread disbelief in matters spiritual. Generations of souls have been taught by science that there is no such thing as a spiritual realm, a Creator, life in the spiritual realm such as angels or demons, or even a human spirit. They are all anti-science so do not exist or have any relevance. All that is left is disbelief which apparently is now deemed scientific.

Disbelief is a gift of no value. Nothing can be done with disbelief. It has no power or purpose. Disbelief prevents self-healing yet that is what mainstream science offers as a scientific position on the spirit. They are blind guides making pronouncements on matters over which they have no understanding.

Disbelief renders souls vulnerable to mental illness, chronic sickness, poverty and misfortune. Pedalling disbelief renders millions of souls spiritually defenceless against pathogens of mental illness and takes away their ability to self-heal.

Millions of souls are condemned to years of mental illness because they cannot summon the power that exists in their spirit, needed to self-heal, because they don't believe the power they have to self-heal even exists. All because mainstream science told them it didn't exist. This is not just an unfortunate mistake, but absolute wickedness.

Mental illness cannot be overcome if there is no belief in the power to overcome it. Belief in the spiritual realm and the Creator is not anti-science but advanced science. Spiritual science operates in a bigger reality than physicists, biologists and chemists can comprehend.

The Dead Sea Scrolls reveal how spiritual science heals mental illness because mental illness is in the spirit. Mainstream science mocks the scrolls despite being unable to heal mental illness. The arrogance is breath-taking. Spiritual science heals where medical science can't. You would think medical science would welcome the opportunity to heal. It doesn't.

Because mainstream science rejects the spirit they have no spiritual knowledge or understanding of death or conception. Thousands of people die everyday and have done from the beginning of time but medical science has no idea what actually happens. This is because death is a separation of the spirit from the body and medical science rejects the existence of the spirit.

I will explain what happens to the soul and spirit after death later. These things are meant to be known by all of us so we will not fear what is to come. Science has stifled this knowledge because it considers anything to do with the spirit to be anti-science when in truth it is advanced science, it is spiritual science, it is what death is all about.

Science is wedded to the theories of one man in the 1850s called Charles Darwin who wasn't even a scientist. The world has changed since the 1850s. Art, music, transport, fashion, healthcare, all transformed beyond recognition except mainstream science and their adherence to the observations of Charles Darwin. Astonishing!

Let us accept for a moment that Charles Darwin, a theologian from the 1800s is right. What would that mean?

It means the Dead Sea Scrolls, a library spanning two thousand years of human history, are wrong. The Creator who curated the Dead Sea Scrolls is also wrong, the Angel of the Presence is wrong, the prophet Enoch is wrong, even though He was there at the time and recorded what he saw.

It means Moses was wrong despite writing down what was dictated to him, word for word, by the Creator Himself. The Messiah Himself, who was crucified for what He knew to be true was also wrong, but Charles Darwin is right.

It is illogical and unscientific to place complete belief in the observations of one man who was not a scientist, nor was he alive when life started on earth. This is the extraordinary position of mainstream science.

We all have the right to believe what we choose. It is called free will. The question is, how do we know our beliefs are true? None of us would knowingly believe something we knew to be untrue.

The question is, how often do we challenge our beliefs? How do we know what we believe is true or not? Most of us accept what we are told unquestioningly. This is not good. We need to test our beliefs, and often. Few do. We shall test all things and hold fast to only that which is good. We shall get to the truth.

The quality of belief is not down to our sincerity for sincerity does not make something true. Christians sincerely believe the Messiah was born at Christmas and His name was Jesus. Sincerity does not make either of those beliefs true. Those sincerely held beliefs are sincerely untrue, lawless and harmful to spiritual health. The quality of belief is dependent on whether it is true or not. Few ever bother to check.

Most of us are taught from a young age to believe things that are not true. How many of us are ever going to check? Politicians, science, religion, academia, and the media rely on our gullibility to sustain their credibility

Let us challenge some beliefs. How old is the planet? Mainstream science cannot agree. Nor can they agree on what it is made of or where it came from. They do not know, so do they tell the truth and say they do not know? No!

Mainstream science teaches that the earth is 4.5 billion years old. A belief that has no evidence to support it. Earth has a crust, a mantle and a core. Another belief with no evidence to support it. We are taught that humans appeared 200,000 years ago somewhere in east Africa creating another belief which cannot be proven.

Eventually we graduate, with hundreds off beliefs that are untested, and untrue. With regard to the spiritual realm, mainstream science offers nothing but disbelief in something that provably exists. It is time to challenge beliefs that have been fed to us, unchallenged, by science and the education system. We need to know what is true and what is not.

Spiritual science, spiritual health and spiritual warfare have been my areas of research for decades. I am not anti-science. I love science. I studied nautical science at Greenhithe Naval College. I love maths and physics. I find no conflict between spiritual science and worldly science because I test everything and hold fast only to that which I find to be true.

The laws of physics, chemistry and biology do not conflict with the laws of the spirit but compliment them. It is the physicists, chemists and biologists who conflict with the laws of spiritual science, not the science itself.

Our earthly realm was created through the spiritual realm, not the other way around. The spiritual realm has more dimensions than our earthly realm, so in that sense is more real than our own dimension.

Somehow mainstream science believes the world runs itself. All those moving part and vast forces without anyone at the helm and yet somehow it all works like a dream and never goes wrong.

Creation is managed by angelic super beings in the heavenly realm. They keep everything in its place and in its time. For the sceptics, who I welcome for scepticism is not a bad thing, I will prove angelic beings exist and manage this earthly realm with meticulous precision for it is provable.

Today, many fear creation is hurtling out of control with no one at the helm. It is not. It is highly regulated, directed and managed. Climate activists sincerely believe planet earth is warming. It is! They believe there will be climate catastrophes. There will be!

Droughts, tsunamis, earthquakes, famines, volcanic eruptions, pandemics, and plagues were all prophesied to come in the last days, thousands of years ago in the scrolls. We were warned in advance. We chose to ignore the warnings and now we panic?

How ironic that the scientists who mock these prophesies are the same scientists who have no idea how to deal with the very things that we were warned of. Science and academia knew best, and apparently still do for they still mock the scrolls.

The scrolls warn of severe droughts, yet the dithering and cowardly leadership of the UK has not created a single new reservoir in over thirty years despite our population increasing by over ten million. Handing responsibility for our water supply over to organisations that are driven by profit is beyond short sighted but absolute stupidity. We have been warned.

Those who are spiritually wise and know of these prophecies have nothing to fear for they will be protected from them.

Mainstream science believes it controls creation. It does not! It has no idea where creation came from, or how, or when. It has no idea how it all goes together, or what propels it. Humankind does not have the codes to creation but was asked to look after the plants and the animals, and we trashed it.

The last thing the Creator will do is leave humankind to oversee His precious creation. What could possibly go wrong with that, I hear you ask?

Prove creation is managed? Let me show you. The Dead Sea Scrolls have hundreds of prophecies foretell history in advance. Some prophecies have been fulfilled exactly as foretold. Others are yet to be fulfilled, some even in our lifetime.

Accurately foretelling what is going to happen in heaven and on earth, proves creation is managed. If it wasn't then the prophecies would not come true. They do, and on time! Someone or something must be managing creation and doing it to a strict timetable.

The point I am making is that prophecies prove history is managed so there must be a Creator. Science says He doesn't exist. Who is telling the truth. Can we trust the scientists? Can we trust the Dead Sea Scrolls? One is lying and one is telling the truth. The scrolls tell us to test all things and hold fast to what is good. Let us test both science and the Dead Sea Scrolls and see where that leads us.

Let us start with science. The humble bumble bee defied scientific explanation by flying. Given its size, weight, shape and wing formation it should not fly according to science. The flying bumble bee was anti-science. Only in this millennium have we understood how.

This proves things exist and thrive that science cannot understand. Things that are anti-science can exist. The laws of spiritual science exist, just like a flying bumble bee, despite science claiming they can't.

Being scientifically inexplicable does not mean it does not exist, it just means it is currently scientifically inexplicable. We are told to follow the science then we will know what is true and what is not. OK, let us follow the science.

Weapons inspector scientists in 2003 followed the science and told us Saddam Hussein had weapons of mass destruction in Iraq. There were none. So maybe this was a one-off and we should not judge the scientific community on one mishap.

In the 1950s, tobacco companies employed scientists to convince the public that there was no link between smoking their cigarettes and getting lung cancer. They assured us smoking was not harmful but could even be good for us because they were following the science.

One famous strap line advert read, 'More doctors smoke Camels than any other cigarette. Medical science was telling us smoking was good for us. And we are supposed to trust science and doctors regarding spiritual health?

In the 1960s scientists told us Thalidomide was a safe drug to alleviate morning sickness for they were following the science. Thalidomide caused many foetal deformities. Sufferers died years later, without receiving any admission of guilt from the pharmaceutical companies, nor an apology or penny compensation. The strap line promoting Thalidomide was, 'now she can cook breakfast again'.

In 2015 the diesel gate scandal exposed scientists, working for car manufacturer VW, fitting a *'defeat device'* to falsify the apparent fuel consumption of their cars. Scientists for VW were paid to deceive and defraud the public yet again leading us to believe they were following the science.

More recently, scientists employed by the pharmaceutical industry reassured us that putting opiates in pain killers would not make them addictive because they are following the science. Many in the USA, who took those painkillers are now struggling with addiction.

The term, 'following the science' is meaningless. It should be 'follow the politics or follow the money.' The point I am making is if you are struggling with disbelief in a Creator because you have been told by science that such beliefs are anti-science, then rethink your belief in the credibility of mainstream science.

According to science, the first law of thermodynamics states that energy cannot be created or destroyed but changes from one form to another. I agree!

Then according to thermodynamics, the human spirit, which is energy, comes from somewhere and goes somewhere. It comes from the spiritual realm and returns to the spiritual realm, just as the Dead Sea Scrolls tell us, in perfect accordance with the first law of thermodynamics.

This is one of many instances where spiritual science parallels physics, chemistry and biology but is still derided by physicists, chemists and biologists.

Medical science cannot create life because life is not chemical, but spiritual. If conception was a chemical process, fertility clinics would offer guarantees. Fertility clinics do not offer guarantees because life is not just a chemical process but a spiritual one over which they have no understanding or control. That is why they offer no guarantees.

Life cannot be made from non-life. No matter how many elements taken from the periodic table and arranged by scientists, they will never create life. Our children are taught in school that life emerged millions of years ago from a primordial soup that somehow had the building blocks of life in it. Another belief being sown into young minds that have no basis in truth or fact and for which there is no evidence.

There is no such primordial soup, nor does humankind have access to the building blocks of life, nor is there any evidence of such a thing. There is no so-called primordial soup from which life emerged because no combinations of any of the elements on earth however combined, can create life. The codes to life are kept far away from humankind. It would be to give the keys of the asylum to the lunatics. I don't think so.

Children are taught that according to science, something, though they know not what, exploded but they know not why, and became all that we see around us today, though they know not how. They don't know what, why, how or when, but the one thing they are certain of is that there is no Creator.

So where did everything come from? Sadly, our children are misled by the education system, become adults engrained with disbelief which is of no benefit whatsoever. If anything, disbelief is an impairment.

The Creator's account of creation is documented within the scrolls which predate science, academia and religion. He was there at the beginning; long before science, academia and religion were even a thing.

By restoring our spirit we can access spiritual power and abilities that are scientifically impossible, such as self-healing and healing others. We can have heightened senses of intuition, empathy, foresight, insight, imagination, creativity, problem solving abilities and astute memory recall.

Ask science to explain any of these supernatural abilities. They can't, despite the fact we all have them. Apparently intuition, foresight, imagination and empathy are all anti-science yet somehow we all have them.

The scrolls document over four thousand years of human history and our interaction with the Creator. We are going to test the scrolls together so you can decide for yourself whether they are credible or not.

Only by testing everything can we get to the truth. Professor Einstein once said that condemnation before an investigation is the height of ignorance. I agree! Dismissing the scrolls as irrelevant without testing them is willing ignorance. Mainstream science is guilty of willing ignorance according to Einstein's own words.

Do not be afraid to test everything. I do! I prove everything I say. Please don't take my word for it, test me back, because I expect nothing less.

Science tells us there is no Creator. Let us test this. If there is proof of a Creator, then where is it? Let me show you.

Living creatures can't reproduce by themselves. Reproduction requires a male and a female which rules out self-replication. If creatures could self-replicate then evolution would be possible. Unfortunately, evolution still doesn't answer the question of where the first creature came from, which brings us back to a Creator.

Life on earth starts with a single cell. No elements on earth can create life so where did that life come from? Life cannot be created from non-life so again, where did our life come from?

63

That single cell must have a spirit within it to give it life. Where does that spirit come from? It is not chemical so cannot come from conception but is spiritual so must come from the spiritual realm. This brings us back to a Creator.

When a single cell of life is created it divides, then divides again and again, forming all the different component parts that go to make up that entire living creature whether it be an elephant, a mouse or a child. Where did all that information on how to make and then assemble all those complex component part come from? This brings us back to a Creator again.

The complexity and communication between all those moving parts is also staggering. The optic nerve from the eye to the brain and how it converts what it sees into knowledge is a miracle in itself, as is the circulatory system and the respiratory system. Somewhere, somehow, there must be a Creator.

And if that was not enough, the single cell decides if it is a male or a female of that species and creates all the necessary component parts for that specific gender. How does it know what gender it is and then how to make all those specific parts? This brings us back to a Creator yet again.

How can evolution account for a male and a female, each with completely different biological structures, perfectly fulfilling the biological needs of the other to procreate. This requires an intelligence that knows the biological structures of both genders of every species on earth, and how they will interact, even before conception. This again leads us to a Creator.

Within a single cell is the entire blueprint of what that creature will become and the ability to physically, chemically and biologically create itself. It knows whether it is a male of the species or a female. Its entirety is somehow known within that single cell. The knowledge is not physically crammed into the single cell but coded in spiritual form within the soul.

Where could all this information come from? Within every spirit is a determined gender, and a lifetime of destiny and potential. How did it get there? The fact that life even exists on a planet that cannot create life itself, proves there must a Creator, for something must have put life there for us to even be here.

No earthly element can create life. Life is spirit so comes from somewhere other than here, because here is not a spiritual realm, it is a physical realm.
Wherever life comes from is where the Creator is. The fact there is life is proof of a Creator.

Procreation requiring a male and a female renders evolution impossible. Where would a partially evolved male or female come from? How would a partially evolved male, and partially evolved female, even procreate? What in heaven's name would they produce? The fact that only fully evolved males and females procreate makes evolution impossible. The impossibility of evolution is what science teaches our children as fact!

The origins of life are purposefully structured to be scientifically inexplicable. That is the point. The Creator's signature is writ large in all the things that are scientifically inexplicable. That is how we can see the works of His hands. His hand is in all that is inexplicable and scientifically impossible, yet somehow exists.

Science cannot tell us which came first the chicken or the egg. The scrolls do. Spoiler alert! It was the chicken. Every creature was created according to its kind, both male and female He made them. Then they procreated. The chicken came first as did the cock, according to its kind, and then they procreated and along came the egg, and they were off, so to speak.

The Dead Sea Scrolls tell us even what day of the week they were created. On the fifth day of creation all the creatures of the sea were made as were all the creatures that fly. Chickens fly so were made on the fifth day.

We know the seventh day of the week is the Sabbath, which is a Saturday, so the fifth day of the week is a Thursday. Not only do the Dead Sea Scrolls tell us what came first, the chicken or the egg, we even know it was on a Thursday. How extraordinary is that?

For those who struggle with disbelief stick with me because we will be testing the prophecies in the Dead Sea Scrolls. You will see for yourself that they are credible and how they came true.

I may have been a little harsh on mainstream science in defence of spiritual science, but I would like to say that there are many excellent scientists who are very decent people, who love their job and do excellent work. I do not criticise you personally.

I challenge the spiritual forces behind mainstream science, not individual scientists. For many individual scientists, I have great respect and mean not to offend. I love science! I studied science. Science reveals the perfection of creation and the hand of the Creator.

RELIGION AND
SPIRITUAL HEALTH

The relationship between religion and spiritual health is awkward to say the least. Religion promises spiritual health but cannot deliver because it does not keep the spiritual laws of life needed for spiritual health.

Religion keeps the traditions of men because it is a worldly power, not a spiritual power. Spiritual health cannot come from worldly power for the spirit does not come from the world.

Spiritual health comes from the spiritual realm and the keys to the Creator in the spiritual realm are in the ten commandments. The Christian and Jewish religions do not keep the ten commandments so don't have the keys to the Creator. By not keeping the commandments their keys unlock Satan for all that is outside the commandments belongs to him.

The great commission of the Church of England was to tend the spiritual health of the nation. Barely 1% of the UK population turns to the Church of England for spiritual health. The Church of England in their defence says that 26 million people, which is over a third of the UK population have been baptised, proving they are fulfilling their great commission.

Unfortunately, infant baptisms have nothing to do with spiritual health. It is like a salesman claiming to be successful because they have thousands of business cards. One is no measure of the other.

Infant baptisms are not in the Bible or the Dead Sea Scrolls or the Torah. Infant baptisms are a tradition of men therefore have no spiritual significance because infants are already sanctified by their innocence. Baptism is a public declaration to keep the laws of the spirit. Infants know nothing of these things so cannot make such a public declaration

That aside, do not judge the Church of England as a failure. It is not. The Church of England is a successful business. It generates nearly a billion pounds a year of income yet barely 1% of the UK population have anything to do with it. That is good business.

67

Church of England Bishops sit in the House of Lords holding sway over the very laws that regulate their business, which is sound corporate practice.

The Church of England cannot serve the government and the Creator at the same time. It is not possible to serve two masters at the same time. Some in the Church of England may be familiar with the scrolls of Matthew and Luke which say,

"No man can serve two masters:
You cannot serve the Creator and mammon."

It is written in Mark 7.8

You have let go of the commandments of Yahuah Elohim,
and chosen the traditions of men.

The Church of England claims to be the custodians of the Bible and protectors of spiritual health in England. To do this they need to keep the ten commandments which they do not keep them. We know the Creator does not work through organised religion because organised religion does not keep His laws.

He works through the souls and spirits of those who do keep the commandments, know Him and belong to Him. He works through His own with whom He does have a relationship. The world often considers those who keep His commandments as foolish.

It is written in 1 Corinthians 27, that the Creator will use the foolish things of the world to confound the wise. He will choose the weak things of the world to put to shame the things which are mighty. He will use the lowly and forgotten in society to expose lawlessness in high places.

He says to us in John 14.15.

If you love me, keep my commandments.

The world also mocks those who keep the commandments as being weak. Did He not say that He will choose the weak things of the world to put to shame the things which are mighty?

The lowly and forgotten are mocked by the worldly for placing their trust in the commandments. Did He not say He will use the lowly and forgotten in society to expose lawlessness in high places?

Two thousand years ago when the Creator was made flesh and dwelt among us, did He become religious? I think not! He became a thorn in the side of religion. He exposed them as hypocrites, liars and deceivers. They then falsely accused Him, had Him flogged, publicly mocked and then crucified. He warns us to keep away from religion for good reason.

Let me show you how it is impossible to keep the commandments and be religious. I think you will be surprised.

The fourth commandment tells us to rest for one day a week: That day is Saturday which is the Sabbath. This commandment originates from the very first week of creation. For those who do not believe creation took seven days to complete, please tell me where the seven-day week comes from? There has never been a time in history when there was not a seven-day week. How do we explain that?

By ignoring the fourth commandment the Church of England ignores the Biblical account of creation, in favour of the pagan Sun's day worship, hence Sunday. It is not the Sabbath, never was nor ever will be. On the first day of the week when the Creator was starting to put everything in creation together, the Church of England takes the day off! Absolutely bonkers!

Obedience to Church doctrines that promise spiritual health, breaks the ten commandments making it harmful to spiritual health. It is like promising to heal someone whilst offering them food that makes them sick. Therein lies the deceit of religion. In their own scriptures the religious are warned countless times, 'take care you are not deceived for many will come in my name.'

The Church of England claims to come in the Creator's name but doesn't even get His name right. They celebrate His birthday on the wrong day and can't even keep His commandments despite the fact there are only ten of them and they have had two thousand years of practice to get it right.

The second commandment forbids icons, effigies or relics in the shape of anything in heaven or on earth to represent the Creator, nor are they to bow down and worship such things for such practices are Satanic.

The Church of England and the Catholic Church have more icons, effigies and relics than anyone else on earth. The pious among them love nothing more than to bow down and devoutly worship them. It is satanic.

Humankind does not have the authority or ability to make anything on earth sacred or Holy. Nor does religion! But hey, when did that ever stop us?

I am a fine-art painter and over the years have produced the occasional competent piece. Far be it for me to deem anything I have produced, ever to be holy. How is it churches are awash with crosses, crucifixes, statues of Mary and the infant Jesus and saints by the dozen, all made by mortal man, yet treated as sacred and holy.

The devout kneel in obedient reverence before these icons and effigies. It is spiritually lawless, generates negative energy and is harmful to the spirit.

Within the spiritual laws of life we are told not to call anyone father except our natural father on earth, and our heavenly Father. What do priests like to be called? 'Father.' This is another example of satanic behaviour presented as religious devotion.

We are told that only the Creator can forgive us of our sins against Him. So how is it Roman Catholic priests and the Pope can offer forgiveness of sins against the Creator, when they are only mortal souls themselves? This is also satanic behaviour presented as religious piety.

The busiest time of year for the church is Christmas. Surely that must be in the commandments and good for spiritual health? Nope! Christmas is not in the Bible, nor is it ordained as a holiday to be celebrated. It is yet another tradition of men. There are many wonderful holidays the Creator does give us to celebrate, but religion prefers to hide those from us forcing us to celebrate the traditions of men instead.

News flash! The Messiah was not born on the 25th of December but on the 4th of June which is the feast of Shavuot. This Holy day falls on a different day each year because it was ordained before the Gregorian calendar that we use today, was instituted.

Christmas is a pagan festival celebrating the sun's winter equinox in the worship of the pagan Sun-God. The ancient scroll of Jeremiah 10.2-4, which is in the Christian Bible, tells Christians not to cut down trees, do not bring them indoors and do not decorate them with gold and silver for that is what pagans do in the worship of their false pagan gods.

Religion hijacked the Bible and removed entire books from it. The congregants are warned not to be deceived, and then their religious doctrines openly deceive them. You could not make this stuff up!

Shepherds do not spend nights out in fields in December. It is winter for heaven's sake! Shepherds are out in the fields at night during the lambing season. The Messiah, who is known by Christians as the lamb of God, was born unsurprisingly in the lambing season which is not in December.

The religious nativity celebrates three wise men who came from the east. Nowhere does it say how many wise men came, but that they had three gifts. The kings of the East did not attend the nativity in the stable but arrived two years later when Joseph, Mary and Yahusha (Jesus) were living in a house. That is why King Herod had all the children up to two years old killed in and around Bethlehem after the wise men of the east had left.

There are Holy days ordained by the Creator that are meaningful and bring health to the spirit. Few know what those holy days are because religion buried them. It is time to restore them which we shall.

So, what of Easter? Surely Easter doesn't break any commandments? I am afraid so. The term Easter comes from Ishtar, the goddess of fertility which is why we have Easter bunnies and Easter eggs.

The original rituals of the goddess Ishtar celebrated fertility. Their Ishtar services included male and female prostitutes who 'served the congregants,' so to speak! Not something we want to see in a Church of England Easter service anytime soon.

We are told not to worship other gods, so paying homage to the false goddess Ishtar breaks another commandment. Christians know worshipping other gods is spiritually harmful, yet willingly break the commandments in obedience to their religion.

Religion promotes infant baptisms. Unfortunately, there is no such thing in the Bible. Such services have no place in the commandments or with spiritual health.

Many turn to religion believing it to be the path to the Creator. This is the great deceit we are warned to beware of for religion does not lead to the Creator but to lawlessness and spiritual destruction.

Religion leads souls away from the Creator. Religious deceit is as old as religion for even the Messiah two thousand years ago warned in the book of Luke, 21.8 where it is written,

"See to it that you are not deceived,
for many will come in my name."

The religious face a dilemma. Do they remain obedient to the doctrines of their religion or obedient to the commandments of the Creator. It is prophesied many will choose religion over the commandments of the Creator. The outcome of that choice will occur on their day of judgement where it is prophesied there will wailing and weeping and gnashing of teeth. Spiritual health is not found in religion, but in a one-to-one relationship with the Creator. This starts with keeping His commandments, for it is written, if you love me, keep my commandments. Spiritual health has nothing to do with religion and everything to do with the ten commandments in the Dead Sea Scrolls.

There are many Christian denominations, all claiming to come in His name so how can they all be right. The Messiah warned us against religion in Matthew, 23.27, when He said,

"Woe to you, teachers of the law
and Pharisees, you hypocrites!

You are like whitewashed tombs, which look beautiful
on the outside but inside, you are full of dead
men's bones and everything unclean."

The Messiah exposed the religious as hypocrites and deceivers. Show me where the Creator or the Messiah is religious! I don't think so. We do not need religion, but we do all need spiritual health.

Many are attracted to religion. I get it. Religious ceremonies can be grandiose and magnificent in their pomp and splendour, attracting many, but remember when substance is gone, all that is left is the ceremony.

Substance does not need ceremonial pomp and splendour for substance has value in and of itself. Our spiritual relationship with the Creator is all substance. There is no need of ceremony for that is but a distraction.

CONCEPTION

Conception is a miracle! It is the moment new life begins on earth. The spirit existed before conception for it was made on the first day of creation.

Conception opens a portal between this world and the heavenly realm. The spirits of humankind are suspended in the heavenly realm, outside time and space, in a state of deep sleep waiting for their predestined moment of conception. This is the moment the human spirit crosses the divide from the spiritual realm to the earthly one and begins life on earth.

At conception the spirit crosses the dimensions and enters the biological cells of the womb. It is the entering of the spirit into the biological cells that gives the biological cells life. Life is spirit, not chemical. Conception has a spiritual dimension as well as a chemical one. We are spiritual beings in physical bodies.

How do we know that the human spirit existed before conception? The Creator revealed this mystery of conception to Jeremiah who wrote,

> *'Before I formed you in the womb I knew you,*
> *before you were born,*
> *I set you apart.'*

The mystery of conception was also revealed to King David, as in David and Goliath, who wrote,

> *You formed my inmost being. You knit me together in my*
> *mother's womb. Thank You, for I am fearfully*
> *and wonderfully made.*

> *Marvellous are Your works. My bones weren't hidden*
> *from you when I was being put together in a secret place,*
> *when I was being woven together in the*
> *deep parts of the earth.*

Conception is a miracle of both the spirit and the flesh. This confounds science who can only see the flesh of conception.

An embryo has life because it has a spirit. That spirit is separate from that of its mother. The embryo may be dependent and connected to the mother, but the spirit of that embryo is distinctly separate and individual from the mother.

Spirits having no molecules do not grow as does an embryo but matures in its quality. It will either be positive and empowered or negative and lawless.

The human spirit has destiny, character, talents skills and a lifetime of potential coded within it. From the moment it leaves the spiritual realm and enters the biological cells in the womb it is a complete human being full of life. The human spirit is made eternal. When it enters the earthly realm it is still eternal by virtue of its innocence.

Our spirit will either remain eternal by forming a relationship with the Creator of our spirit, or should we choose to reject Him, be destined to eternal destruction on our day of judgement. The purpose of free will is to choose eternal life.

Every spirit is unique, precious and made in the image of the Creator. Twins may be identical physically but they are separate and unique spiritually. Conjoined twins are also separate spiritually. Each human soul is unique and perfect, made in the image of the Creator.

DEATH
AND THE HUMAN SPIRIT

Death is often feared because it is shrouded in mystery. Death should not be feared but something to prepare for and enter with confidence. The journey we make when we die is revealed in the scrolls and should reassure us. Religion and science have their own narratives about death neither of which make any sense.

Science and religion can only guess what happens after death because they have not ventured beyond the veil and returned to say what is there. The account we are given in the in the scrolls is by the Angel of the Presence, Uriel, who is there in the underworld and oversees Sheol, to where we descend upon death. This process has been highly regulated from the beginning when Cain first killed Abel and the process will not change until the end of this age.

Uriel and his team are responsible for guiding the spirits of the deceased into their place of rest. We are told these mysteries so we should not fear death but prepare for it in advance.

When the physical body dies, it does not take the spirit with it. The body, as in the flesh, returns to dust from whence it came and is no more.

The spirit continues to exist. Our spirit has no molecules so what is there in it or of it to die? Nothing! It is not physical so how can it decay with the body? It can't which is why it continues to exist, for it is spiritual energy that is separate from the physical body. It lives on, but how and where?

Science confirms through the laws of thermodynamics that energy cannot just die or disappear. It must go somewhere. It does!

The spirit separates from the body upon death, for one is physical and one is spiritual. The spiritual part of us descends into a place where it can rest in peace, which is where we get the initials on tombstones, *'RIP'*.

Archangel Uriel and his vast team oversee the souls of the deceased as they descend into great caverns of peace, within the depths of the earth. Here they rest and await their day of judgement. Those who keep the commandments await judgement without fear but with reassurance and expectation of an eternal life to come.

The mystery of death is knowable. The meaning of life cannot be understood without understanding the mystery of death. That is why the Angel of the Presence was instructed to teach us these mysteries. We are to live meaningful lives, thrive and prosper, and enter death with reassured expectation of eternal life.

Life and death are as much a process of creation as sunrise and sunset are. The processing of deceased souls are managed by entities in the spiritual realm.

We did not get ourselves here from the spiritual realm through our own efforts, yet here we are. Most have no idea where they came from or where they go, so it is no wonder they are fearful. It need not be so. Those who know the truth have no fear. This is the reason we were given the wisdom of the scrolls in the first place.

Understanding life, death and the judgement of our soul by the laws of the ten commandments enables us to live lawful lives of abundance, fulfilling the contribution we were born to make in this life and rest in peace with every expectation of life in the next age.

Many pass away without any understanding. Had they been wise, many souls would have lived very different lives and made very different choices. If they had understanding, many would have received eternal life. For those who are deceased, it is too late. For it is written, 'my people perish through lack of knowledge.'

So, what happens when we die? There are great caverns within the earth overseen by angelic beings appointed to minister to the souls of the deceased. They guide the souls of the deceased to a place where they may *rest in peace.'*

This is where we get the initials on tombstones, *'RIP'* and the concept of going downwards. The earth is not solid rock, nor does it have a crust, a mantle and core, but is a complex structure with layered configurations of rock, oil, gas, coal, peat, shale, huge cave systems, oceans of water, molten lava, moving tectonic plates, sinkholes, hydrothermal vents and great abysses. Planet earth has a highly complex internal structure.

Science does not know what the earth is made of. Let me show you. The diameter of the earth is 7,917.5 miles, which gives it a radius of 3,958 miles. That means from the earth's surface to its core is 3,958 miles. The deepest borehole ever drilled is the Kola Superdeep borehole in the Pechengsky District in Russia. No one has gone deeper into the earth's surface than this borehole.

It is 7.58 miles deep. That is 7.58-miles of penetration into a planet 3,958 miles thick to its core. That is in mathematical terms 0.2% which is to barely scratch the surface.

To embark on a journey of nearly four thousand miles and do only seven and a half miles of it is to have very little idea what is on that journey. I invite any scientist to explain to me how they know what is within the earth when less than 0.2% of It has been explored?

You can decide whether 0.2% of evidence is conclusive or not. I would not agree to or invest in something I knew only 0.2% about. If a surgeon told me he was going to operate on me with only 0.2% likelihood of success I would sit that one out.

If the prophecies in the Dead Sea Scrolls were only 0.2% accurate rather than 100% accurate, science would be right to mock them. They are astonishingly accurate yet still they are mocked. When science applies evidence to their own beliefs, apparently 0.2% of evidence is conclusive. Really!

Christians believe when they die, they go to heaven. Not wishing to disappoint or offend, but nowhere in the Bible does it say that. Deceased souls going up to heaven is another tradition invented by men that has no truth or fact. No one goes anywhere until after the judgement and even then, Heaven comes here not the other way round. Check the Lord's Prayer: It says,

Our Father who art in heaven, hallowed be thy name. Thy Kingdom 'come;' thy will be done 'on earth' as it is in Heaven. A new heaven comes down to a new earth after the day of judgement. Not the other way round. Nowhere does it say we go there.

The idea that some souls go to heaven and others don't, means souls are judged. There would have to be a day of judgement every day of the week because people die every day of the week. That is a ridiculous concept.

Every day is not a day of judgement because we are all going to be judged together, at the same time, on the last day. That will be the day of judgement for all of us.

Judgement determines who receives eternal life and who doesn't. The souls found wanting are thrown into the lake of eternal fire and will cease to exist. Judgment is a serious business that we are expected to prepare for because it is the reason for life on earth. It is the meaning of life.

When we rest in peace, there is no concept of time. Vast caverns deep within the earth are layered one beneath another. Human souls occupy the top three layers in accordance with the quality of their lives.

The highest chamber is for the souls who knew the Creator and will receive eternal life. The layer below is for those who were martyred for the Creator, and they also receive eternal life. Below them is the biggest chamber where the deceased souls of those who rejected the ten commandments, rest in peace. They will cease to exist after their day of judgement.

Further below are the caverns of darkness and condemnation. They are places of incarceration for fallen angels who violated the laws of creation.

This is also where 90% of the demons, the spiritual pathogens behind mental illness, are incarcerated.

Only 10% of demons who ever lived are free to roam on earth to torment humankind. This deep dark chamber of incarceration is known as the 'Abyss of Condemnation'. The chambers of the underworld are known in Hebrew as 'Sheol' or 'Tartarus' in Greek.

For souls who are 'RIP,' resting in peace, there is no concept of time, pain or suffering. It is not hell with flaming fires, torture, and pain. The flaming fire spoken of is the lake of eternal fire which is below the Abyss of Condemnation where fallen angels are incarcerated. The cover to the lake of eternal fire will not be removed until the day of judgement.

There is no such thing as hell, or purgatory or eternal damnation as they are inventions of the Roman Catholic Church designed to frighten souls into religious obedience. There are huge caverns within the earth and deep abysses even deeper and even further down lies the lake of eternal fire.

This will be uncovered on the day of judgement. Everything found wanting on the day of judgement, according to the lives they have lived, humankind, angels and demons, will be cast into it and exist no more. This may sound harsh and frightening. It is meant to. Judgement is serious. Ignore it at your peril.

There is no devil in the underworld. Sheol is meticulously managed by the Archangel Uriel and his team. It runs perfectly.

The scrolls state that wisdom starts with a fear of Yahuah Elohim. Many ask, what kind of loving God wants us to fear Him? They misunderstand. We are not to fear the Creator of heaven and earth because He loves us. We are to fear His judgement upon us for breaking His laws, the same laws He gave to us in the beginning.

What laws? The spiritual laws science and academia have hidden and mock. The same laws religion has edited and rewritten. I am talking about the ten commandments.

The judgement and its consequences have been made known to humankind from the beginning, even in the scroll of Enoch, which is the first book ever written. It is amazing how wise we become when we know that we will account for the life we have lived. Sadly, many reject this wisdom, convinced there is no judgement. Someone is going to be in for a shock and I don't think it is me.

It is not the Creator's fault if humankind rejects Him, His judgement and its consequences. On that day many will be stricken with panic, fear, weeping and gnashing of teeth. We have all been given free will to choose the life we have lived. Come our day of judgement we cannot say, we didn't know!

Those who are saved live on earth after the judgement as members of the Creator's family, with Him, forever. That is what is meant in the Lord's Prayer when it says, 'thy kingdom come, thy will be done on earth as it is in heaven.' Heaven comes to earth after the judgement, and we receive spiritual bodies that never age. What is not to like about eternal life?

Wisdom brings peace and empowerment to the soul because wisdom is a fruit of the spirit. Spiritually empowered people thrive. They do not fear death nor judgement for they know what is to come and prepare for it, as part of their destiny.

The moment we die there is nothing we can do to change the life we have lived. The fate of our judgement is sealed according to that life. The die is cast, eternally.

Wisdom teaches us to focus on the quality of life we are living now because that is something we can control, change and improve. The religious will not be saved by their religion. The life we are living now is the life on which we will be eternally judged so let's make it a lawful one rather than a religious one.

You can reject wisdom, but if you do, do not complain at the outcome awaiting you on the day of judgement. I do not wish to scare you, but it is better to share the truth with you today, than to hide these things from you, only for you to discover them when it is too late.

I will share the spiritual laws of life with you so you will have the opportunity to choose between what is lawful and what is not. You are free to choose your spiritual path. It is your life you are living, not mine.

You need not perish on the day of judgement through lack of knowledge as many are prophesied to do. This book gives you the knowledge to choose wisely.

Eternal life awaits those who choose eternal life, eternal death awaits those who choose eternal death. It is not complicated, but it is eternal. Restoring the health of your spirit is a matter of life and death, eternal life and death to be precise.

It does not get bigger or more important than that. Your eternal future is completely in your hands. Choose well dear friend and I look forward to seeing you on the other side, eternally.

ANIMAL SPIRITS
AND HUMAN SPIRITS

Fig. 4

DEVONSHIRE HARE
Painting by Rosa-Lee Tuffney

Human spirits are unlike animal spirits because human spirits are made in the image of the Creator. Animal spirits are not. Humans can know the Creator and enter a covenant relationship with Him. Animals can't.

The Creator made humans in His image so He may have an eternal family, living with Him on earth, in the age to come. Some souls alive today will live forever with the Creator here on earth.

They will have eternal bodies and live an eternal life. They are those who believe in, and learnt of, the Creator and His purpose for humankind. In short, those who have spiritual health.

Eternal life is offered to all of us. No one is denied the opportunity to live forever. This is the purpose of free will which we have all been given. It is all about the life we choose to live and the beliefs we choose to hold. Animals do not have free will but are driven by instinct. Spiritually, animal spirits are very different from human spirits.

Those who choose eternal life become like angels who also have eternal life. The big difference between humans and angels is that no matter how powerful, eternal or close to the Creator they may be, they can never be part of His family. Neither angels nor animals can be part of the Creator's family. Humans can. The Messiah did not die on the cross for animals or for angels, but for humankind.

Animals are created for companionship, pleasure and to ease our burden; for originally they were not meant to be eaten. We may love them as family but spiritually they are not family. Animals cannot recognise creation as a gift from the Creator nor can they know the Creator's plans and purpose for creation. We can.

The idea we evolved from apes because apes share certain physical characteristics is spiritual nonsense and without basis in science. There is no evidence to support the idea that we evolved from apes or any other creature, nor has any other creature evolved from us. Each species is created according to its kind. Each species shall procreate according to its kind.

Evidence exists disproving human evolution from apes but is hidden to protect Darwin's theory of evolution. In 1912 the Natural History Museum in London presented fossilised bones of an apparent single skeleton that was part ape and part human. It was presented as the missing link proving humans evolved from apes.

The fossils were known as the *'Piltdown Man'*. Finally, the debate could be put to rest. The argument had been settled. Evolution was a real thing. Or was it?

In 1953 it was confirmed that the 'Piltdown Man' was a hoax. Why would the Natural History Museum in London perpetrate a hoax? Why would they lie about evolution if they believed it was true? Mainstream science perpetrated this hoax to protect the theories of evolution. If they believed evolution was true, why the hoax? Exactly! Having been exposed as a hoax, the scientists then went to great lengths to cover it up.

In 1974 another hoax proving evolution from apes was foisted on the public in the form of a skeleton called Lucy. The knee joint was found three kilometres away from the rest of the skeleton, seventy meters lower in the ground and discovered sometime earlier. When challenged Dr Johansen admitted it did not come from Lucy but a similar species so could be connected to Lucy. This level of guesswork and speculation is staggering.

The laws of creation state each creature is made according to its kind and will procreate according to its kind. Dogs have remained dogs and cats have remained cats despite living side by side for thousands of years. Neither dogs nor cats have merged into dats or cogs or evolved into anything else. Scientists cannot grasp this law of creation despite having empirical proof that it is so.

Species do not evolve out of, or into other species. If this were so we would have seen it and science would have the evidence. They would be shouting it from the roof tops for it would undermine the Creator. We have not seen it and science has presented no evidence to challenge this law of creation.

Animals are not vulnerable to mental illness in the same way humans are. Mental illness is caused by spiritual pathogens attacking the spirit. Spiritual pathogens feed off negative energy caused by humans breaking spiritual laws.

Animals have no concept of spiritual laws, are not subject to them so cannot break them. This means they do not generate negative energy on which spiritual pathogens can feed. The spiritual energy of an animal is of a different quality because it is not regulated by the ten commandments. The spiritual energy of humankind is.

Therefore, we do not see mental illness among animals in the wild. They are not known to self-harm or have eating disorders, or suffer depression, compulsive, obsessive or addictive behaviour, or commit suicide.

Spiritual pathogens can enter animal spirits it they choose. In the scroll of Matthew it is recorded that the Messiah healed a mentally ill man, possessed by demons, who lived among the tombs in the region of the Gerasene's.

When the spiritual pathogens were being cast out they pleaded with the Messiah to be allowed to enter a herd of pigs rather than being totally disembodied. The Messiah allowed it and the demons went into the spirits of swine. The herd of swine then ran over the cliff into the sea of Galilee and drowned taking the demons with them.

DESTINY

Destiny is not the same as fate. Fate is lawless whereas destiny is the highest spiritual purpose a soul can have. Leaving things to fate is to leave things to chance. Those without spiritual health have only fate to guide them, those with spiritual health can know their destiny and follow it. Destiny gives life purpose and direction.

Spiritual health reveals our true destiny. Every life has purpose and direction though many never discover what it is. Those who know their destiny know where they are going and have the tools they need in the fruits of their spirit to get there. They thrive and succeed.

We are all given a unique set of talents, skills and personality traits, all of which are needed to reach our destiny. None of us are put here by accident. None of us are surplus. We all have a unique contribution to make to this world. We are destined to make that contribution.

Amazing contributions throughout history were destined to happen. We know this because prophecies tell us what to expect and when. Those breakthroughs and advancements were written into the spirits of those destined to make those contributions on the first day of creation when all the spirits were created. Everyone is destined to contribute for we are all born to succeed. Part of the joy of living and the meaning of life is discovering what our contribution is meant to be, and then fulfilling it.

The key is spiritual health. When we know what our talents and skills are, when we can see the fruits of our spirit, we can see the path and the direction in life we are born to follow. That is to know our destiny.

Someone who loves to swim is born to swim, someone who loves animals is born to be with animals. When you do what you love for a living you will never do a day's work in your life because you are doing what you are born to do. I paint and I teach spiritual health! I fight demons in the spiritual realm helping people to overcome mental illness because it is what I am born to do. You too have a contribution to make. The fun is discovering what it is.

Mental illness robs us of spiritual health. We lose our talents and skills. We lose sight of our destiny. We cannot see the direction or purpose to our life.

Sadly, many never discover what they were born to do. They never pursued their talents and skills because they never connected to their spirit. Many pass away in old age never knowing the amazing contribution they were born to make.

Only you can make your contribution. The world is waiting for you to make it. Your contribution is as exclusive to you as mine is to me. Destiny is about finding your life's purpose and journey. If you do not know the purpose or meaning of your life, then your spirit needs some care and attention.

We all have talents. Talents bring us joy, confidence and self-esteem, which are fruits of the spirit. Singers love to sing as chefs love to cook and artists love to paint. The world generously rewards the talented. We are all talented, but many never bother to find out what their talents are. No one can say that they have no talent, for what they really mean is that they have not bothered to find out what talents they truly have.

Others who know they have talents choose lives where those talents are never used. They never make the unique contribution to the world they were born to make for they never used their talents. They never become the great success they were born to be.

Life is not a rehearsal. There is no second time around for those who don't do so well the first time. This is it, so make it count! Discover your talents and use them to find the unique contribution you are born to make to this world. Your talents will lead to your contribution so develop them and see where it leads.

In old age many poor souls knew in their spirit something was missing, life felt unfinished. The end came too soon. They expected more because there was more. They once saw destiny in their dreams but did nothing about it. Their destiny never happened because they never grabbed it and ran with it.

Their contribution remained incomplete. They lacked courage. With a healthy spirit they would have had all the courage they needed for courage is a fruit of the spirit. This is how a neglected spirit in poor health can rob us of our destiny.

A life where our talents and skills are not needed or appreciated is to be living the wrong life. Doing things for which we have no talent is a joyless existence. Leave those things to someone who enjoys doing them for no matter how joyless the task, there is somebody out there who will love doing it. Thankfully for me there are people out there who love housework.

Discover your talents and use them, that is why you have them. You are more extraordinary than you could ever imagine and never more so than when you discover your talents and follow them to your true destiny.

SYMPTOMS
OF A SPIRIT IN NEGLECT

The spirit may be invisible, but the symptoms of its neglect are not. We see the symptoms of spiritual neglect as mental illness, chronic sickness, emotional instability, conflict with others, lack of confidence and self-worth, poverty and misfortune. These are all symptoms of a spirit in neglect.

Quality of life is directly connected to the health of the spirit. The keys to restoring our fortunes in life lie in the health of our spirit. Misfortune is not a mandatory part of life but is the outcome of negative spiritual energy. Misfortune is avoidable and can be overcome through the art of spiritual warfare.

We can redirect misfortune and create good fortune through spiritual warfare. Fruits of the spirit such as intuition, empathy, insight and foresight can be used as protection from misfortune and enable us to thrive. That is what the fruits of the spirit are for. Without them we cannot fend misfortune off or thrive.

A spirit in poor health leads us to repeat the same mistakes in life over and over, trapping us in cycle of struggle and hardship. Whatever we try, life just doesn't seem to get any better. Life will not improve until the health of the spirit Is restored. Spirit heals spirit as flesh heals flesh. If misfortune is rooted in the spirit, healing the spirit will overcome misfortune, whereas medicating the body won't.

Healing the spirit breaks the hold of misfortune and poor mental health. With a healthy spirit we can overcome loneliness, rejection, guilt, shame, addiction, poor relationships, loss of confidence, loss of self-esteem, regret, infertility, phobias, irrational beliefs, suicidal tendencies, and chronic physical health conditions.

The health of the spirit affects every area of our life for it is the essence of who we are. There is nothing we can do that doesn't involve our spirit which is why when it is adversely affected there is no part of our life that isn't also adversely affected.

No one is exempt from the symptoms of a neglected spirit, not even the rich and famous. Money, fame and power are no protection from the symptoms of poor spiritual health.

So, what are the benefits of a healthy spirit? A healthy spirit bears fruit. Fruits of the spirit include peace of mind, contentment, gratefulness, patience, kindness, confidence, creativity, imagination, empathy, the ability to heal and self-heal, courage, confidence and self-belief to name just a few spiritual fruits.

The fruit of a healthy spirit improves our ability to interact with the world around us, and how we treat those we love. Our life is transformed. Fruits of the spirit are fundamental to our personality and character, two big factors that govern our quality of life.

That is why our personality and character changes when we are struggling with mental health issues.

Horrible people who treat the world around them horribly, bring upon themselves horrible lives whereas those who treat others, and the world around them kindly, find others and the world around them treating them kindly too.

When we treat the world differently, so the world treats us differently. Treating the world around us better leads to life becoming easier, happier and more successful. The fruits of the spirit enable us to treat others and the world around us very skilfully.

Now we know what the symptoms of a neglected spirit are, let us look at the fruits of the spirit and the kind of life they are going to bring to us.

FRUITS
OF THE SPIRIT

Fruits of the spirit are supernatural abilities that we all have but are mostly overlooked. The human spirit, being spiritual energy, operates beyond the natural world. Things outside the natural world are supernatural. Our spirit operates outside the natural world bringing us supernatural abilities.

Courage, loyalty, trustworthiness, reliability, integrity, decency, patience, self-belief, self-discipline, mental and emotional resilience, confidence, imagination, creativity, and kindness were once celebrated as pillars of aa person's character. They were once the measure of a man or a woman. Today they are largely ignored.

A healthy spirit bears a lot of fruit and a fruitful life is abundant and joyous. A fruitless life is far harder.

Spiritual fruits are made from positive energy. Mental illness by contrast is made from negative energy. This is why fruits of the spirit disappear during mental illness.

Mental illness is devoid of kindness, patience, empathy and generosity toward others, loyalty, trustworthiness, reliability, integrity, self-discipline, confidence, imagination, and creativity all of which are fruits of the spirit. Loss of spiritual fruits during mental illness proves mental illness is a disease of the spirit and not the body. Mental illness is negative energy for if it was positive, the fruits would not be lost.

Fruits of the spirit help us navigate life. With them life is joyous, peaceful and abundant. Without them life is hard to navigate. Let us look at the fruits of the spirit to see what I mean.

- INTUITION
- EMPATHY
- INSIGHT
- FORESIGHT
- SELF-HEALING AND HEALING OTHERS
- EXCEPTIONAL MEMORY RECALL
- CREATIVITY AND IMAGINATION
- ENHANCED PROBLEM-SOLVING SKILLS
- REVELATION
- CONFIDENCE
- SELF BELIEF
- MENTAL AND EMOTIONAL RESILIENCE
- COURAGE

This list is far from complete. There are many more fruits of the spirit such as kindness, patience, contentment, gratefulness, generosity and discernment. We shall consider the big ones first. Without fruits of the spirit life is difficult, with them it is easier.

INTUITION

Intuition is the ability to understand something instinctively, without the need for conscious reasoning. We do not need to work it out, we just *'get it.'* Intuition is faster than the speed of thought. To intuit what is happening around us can quickly steer us away from trouble. Intuition can protect us from toxic relationships. Intuitive people have a supernatural inbuilt warning system to protect them. They do not go through life constantly bumping into things for their intuition steers them away.

EMPATHY

Empathy is the highest level of communication between living souls. Empathy is to feel what another sentient being is feeling without being told or shown. It is faster than language or reason. Empathy is supernatural. Let me give you an example of empathy on a supernatural level.

I have twin brothers, Nicholas and Simon. When they were about seven years old, one was at our house in Mereworth in Kent and the other was at our grandparent's house in Wimbledon, London. They were separated by 36 miles.

Simon was attacked by an Alsatian dog and badly bitten. At the same time, Nicholas, who was in London, had a panic attack. He demanded to speak immediately to Simon, his twin brother, on the phone. Nicholas was somehow experiencing a level of emotional trauma directly connected to that of his twin brother Simon, who was 36 miles away.

This level of empathy is not unnatural or uncommon, but supernatural and commonplace. Empathy is a fruit of the spirit. It is especially strong among siblings, particularly twins and triplets. Families are connected spiritually with supernatural levels of empathy that differs from that of friends. Family members don't have to like each other to have this level of empathy. It is spiritual not emotional.

Science cannot explain it. I love science, especially quantum physics and mechanics. Similar inexplicable connections of empathy appear to exist between photons of light. Let me explain.

Photon particles were divided and separated from each other by several miles in the Hadron Collider at Cern. Conditions surrounding only one particle were changed, yet both particles, separated by several miles, reacted similarly to the change in conditions. The behaviour of the photon particles was like that observed between my twin brothers. The photons of light appear to show a bizarre form of empathy.

Everything in creation appears to be connected having a form of empathy with everything else. We are part of a vast integrated matrix.

INSIGHT

Insight enables us to understand circumstances or the motivations of others with supreme accuracy. Knowing where we stand, who we can trust and what to anticipate gives us a supernatural level of awareness and protection. Insight enables us to sense trouble long before it reaches us smoothing our journey through life.

FORESIGHT

Being able to predict the future makes expecting the unexpected much easier. Foresight is not gambling or guesswork, wishful thinking or imagination. Foresight is to see ahead of time the direction of things to come with a high degree of probability. What is expected may not have happened yet, but it is felt in the spirit that it will. It is to know history in advance. Foresight is a gift that becomes more accurate and reliable the more it is used.

HEALING

We have the power to self-heal physically, mentally and spiritually. We also have the power to heal others. Sadly, most have forgotten their spirit has this ability. Losing contact with our spirit means we have lost our ability to self-heal or heal others. Spiritual health restores this supernatural ability and reminds us that we have this extraordinary skill.

ENHANCED MEMORY

Every experience we have ever had is stored in our subconscious. A neglected spirit buries them. A healthy spirit restores them. Enhanced memory is a fruit of the spirit. We can recall everything that has ever happened to us. It is all there in the subconscious.

In near-death experiences many say their life flashed before them. This is possible because their whole life is recorded in the subconscious. With a healthy spirit it can be accessed. Hypnotherapists access parts of the subconscious to regress people back in time during therapy. With a healthy spirit, we can do this ourselves.

CREATIVITY AND IMAGINATION

Creativity and imagination are fruits of the spirit. Children are extremely creative and imaginative. They have a lot of fruit because their spirits are young, innocent, and healthy. As the health of the spirit wanes so do fruits like creativity and imagination.

Ask a class of eight-year-olds if they can sing, dance and paint. They will all say yes. Ask the same class when they are sixteen years old and far fewer will say yes. The spirit is already in decline.

Many, lost in creativity and imagination lose all track of time. What feels to them like a few minutes is often many hours. That is because creativity and imagination are rooted in the spirit. The world is shaped by creativity and imagination, as was creation itself.

PROBLEM-SOLVING SKILLS

To hypothesise is to imagine outcomes to complex problems as a strategy to find solutions to the problems. Those with imagination hypothesise easily. Today it is called modelling or forecasting and used to predict outcomes to problems. Spiritually healthy people are far better equipped to hypothesise and think outside the box than those with neglected spirits. Spiritually healthy souls have a supernatural advantage to solving problems.

REVELATION

A revelation is to have instant insight into a truth. Truths are like laws that hold creation together. Isaac Newton had a revelation into gravity and for those who are curious or love science, here it is. ($F=Gmm/r^2$).

Archimedes had a revelation, a eureka moment which gave us the Archimedes principle being ($Fb =-pgV$). Einstein had revelations such as ($E=mc^2$). We can all have revelations, moments of mental clarity if we have a spirit healthy enough to receive them. They are sudden, complete, and on reflection often seem obvious. Revelations can appear in our dreams. Revelation is a fruit of the spirit.

CONCLUSION
TO FRUITS OF THE SPIRIT

Other fruits include confidence, self-belief, self-esteem, courage, mental and emotional resilience, contentment, joy, happiness, gratefulness, patience, kindness, abundance, generosity, loving relationships, life-long friendships, and more.

These gifts are meant for all of us for they are embedded in every spirit and part of our human nature. Imagine having an abundance of these fruits in your life now. How different would life be?

Fruits of the spirit guide us to the life we are supposed to live no matter how far off course we have wandered. As the spirit is healed, so it bears fruit, more plentiful than ever. Be assured, your best life is still to come.

THE SPIRIT
OF THE CREATOR

Our spirit is a living entity. It exists which means it was created. We have a Creator. Our Creator also has a spirit. Our spirit is made in His image. This means He knows each one of us, and each of us has the capacity to know Him.

Through His laws we can connect with Him spiritually. We can know what is lawful and what is not. This makes humans unique among creatures on earth. But why would we want to draw close to the Creator? What can He do for us? He can transform our lives no matter how broken they are, for He said,

"Take My yoke upon you and learn from Me, for I am gentle and lowly in heart, and you will find rest for your souls."

Those who believe and learn of Him are those He reveals Himself to and gives rest to their souls. We cannot know Him or draw close to Him without His laws. We learn of Him through His laws. The more we learn the closer we draw. The more we know and understand of Him, the more reason we have to believe in Him. We cannot believe in things we know nothing about or do not understand.

The spirit of the Creator can dwell within the human spirit. The stronger our belief in the Creator the more His spirit will dwell within ours and the stronger our spirit becomes. Spiritual health is restored and sustained by our relationship with our maker. The deeper the relationship the more resilient our spiritual health.

When the Creator's spirit indwells, it changes the spiritual DNA of that human spirit. It is as if the human spirit is renewed or reborn. It is no longer the same.

The spirit of the Creator is known as the Holy Spirit, or in Hebrew, the 'Ruach ha Kodesh', which means the Breath of life. In the beginning, the Creator breathed life into Adam's nostrils. Life is a spiritual force that can only come from the Creator. The Creator's spirit can indwell the spirits of those who believe in Him. That is the power of belief.

The Ruach ha Kodesh is not an 'it,' but a He! He is a spiritual person. He is a powerful entity with a personality. He is omniscient, omnipresent and omnipotent, meaning He is all-knowing, ever-present and all-powerful. He has emotions and can be grieved when we break the commandments and delighted when we keep them.

He does not have a name in the same way the Creator and His Son have names. He has a title, the Breath of Life, the Holy Spirit or the Ruach ha Kodesh.

The Ruach ha Kodesh connects us to the Creator. We do not need to pray to Him or worship Him for our relationship is directly with the Creator, and His Son.

The Ruach ha Kodesh equips us for spiritual warfare. He is the big gun we need against the spiritual pathogens of mental illness. Spiritual pathogens cannot stand against the Ruach ha Kodesh. When the Ruach ha Kodesh dwells with in us, the spiritual pathogens cannot stand.

The Ruach ha Kodesh gives us the power to self-heal and to heal others. When He indwells our spirit, angelic beings see us and are appointed to protect and minister to those with the Ruach ha Kodesh within them. This is the concept of the guardian angel.

Those with the Ruach ha Kodesh are called the Yahudim, meaning those who are saved. I explain the meaning and relevance of this ancient Hebrew word later. It is a wonderful mystery unto itself.

The Ruach ha Kodesh strengthens us and causes our spirit to bear fruit. We become the highest versions of ourselves we can be. How do we invite the Ruach ha Kodesh to dwell within us? We start by keeping the 10 commandments which we will look at later.

As we learn who the Creator is through the ten commandments, we will discover much to believe in. With wisdom and understanding comes a stronger and deeper belief. The stronger the belief, the stronger the spirit, the more the fruit, the higher the quality of life. What is not to like?

CHAPTER 3
THE FORCES
BEHIND MENTAL ILLNESS

WHAT ARE
SPIRITUAL PATHOGENS?

Pathogens are organisms that bring disease to the body. Spiritual pathogens are entities that bring disease to the spirit. Disease in the spirit is not physical, has no mass or molecules nor does it exist physically but is negative spiritual energy. It behaves like a disease but is spiritual energy in substance and form.

Disease of the spirit is curable through the spirit as disease of the flesh is curable through the flesh. A disease of the spirit is not curable through the body because a disease of the spirit is not in the body. Medicating the body for a condition that is in the spirit does not lead to a cure. Spirit heals spirit as flesh heals flesh.

Spiritual pathogens are entities of negative energy that feed off negative energy. They cannot tolerate positive energy. I will show you how to generate positive energy to overcome the negative energy behind mental illness.

Negative energy comes from dark negative thoughts and beliefs whereas positive energy comes from light positive thoughts and beliefs. The quality of spiritual energy affecting our daily lives is dependent on the quality of the thoughts and beliefs we choose to dwell on.

Replacing negative thoughts with bigger, more powerful positive thoughts is how we overcome the pathogens behind mental illness. This is not easy to do by ourselves in our own strength, but with this book and the hidden power in the ten commandments it is possible.

Negative energy lies in thoughts such as jealousy, anger, spite, rejection vengeance and betrayal. Allowing such thoughts to get a foothold in our mind brings nothing but trouble and can open the door to mental illness or chronic sickness. Spiritual warfare is about keeping those harmful thoughts far away for as the adage goes,

'What we think about we bring about.'

Spiritual pathogens seek to control our thoughts and beliefs to gain control of our body. When they do they are no longer disembodied for they can express their wickedness and harmful malevolence through our body. Their aim is to destroy us. Taking control of our body through mental illness enables them to harm us.

Driving a human soul to commit suicide or murder is their ultimate aim for taking a life is the greatest offence to the Creator. Every life is created in His image, every life belongs to Him and He took pleasure in making every one of us. Suicide or murder is to take what is most precious to Him for we are His greatest achievement. He tells us we are His masterpiece, His poema, (poem).

Separating a soul from others, bringing misery, sadness, rejection, pain, hopelessness and suffering are all aspects of the pathogen's play list. Malevolence is their nature, and it is by their malevolence we identify them and separate ourselves from them, and ultimately overcome them.

We overcome the wickedness of pathogens by raising the quality of our thoughts and beliefs. Thinking, believing and speaking the Creator's own words and laws aloud generates immense amounts of positive energy. Pathogens cannot tolerate positive energy for it is like shining a light in the darkness. It is written that,

The light shines in the darkness

but the darkness cannot comprehend nor overcome it.

In days past people would commonly speak the ten commandments aloud knowing the power they held. They would also speak the psalms, parables and proverbs aloud knowing they too had immense spiritual power. Today this power is forgotten. Seldom is the spiritual power of the spoken word used. I will teach you how to restore this power and use it to great effect for it is the front line of spiritual warfare.

Occultists know the power of the spoken word, reciting incantations, spells, chants and curses. Religion too as they get the congregants to recite texts from the Book of Common Prayer.

Red Indians would dance and chant round the fire as would many African tribal people. Buddhists, Hindu's, Sikh's and Muslims all have their chants and Christians have their Taizé chants set to music. Chants and incantations have immense spiritual power because there is power in the spoken word. We cover this hidden power in more detail later. It is an intriguing subject.

Negative and positive thoughts cannot exist in our mind, side by side, at the same time any more than it can be light and dark at the same time. It is not possible to think positive and negative thoughts simultaneously.

The commandments lead our thoughts and beliefs into positive territory. We cannot be in positive territory and negative territory at the same time. Negative energy cannot follow us into positive territory. This is how the ten commandments wrap a layer of protection around us.

Without negative energy in our thoughts and beliefs, there is nothing for the pathogens to feed off. They die because there is nothing to sustain them.

Modern life is awash with negative energy. It flows continuously from the movies, social media, video games and entertainment. Enactments of murder, violence, death, destruction, betrayal, greed, pornography, suffering, torture, warfare, injustice and cruelty is now considered entertainment. Even comedy relies on profanity or lewdness to get a laugh. We are drowning in negative energy completely unaware of what it is doing to our spiritual health and quality of life.

Young minds today have little or no hope of discerning what is negative and what is not for they are being fed negative energy as a staple diet. They are the most vulnerable generation to mental illness ever, and it is as if no one cares.

Mental illness is always harmful. Whoever heard of a mental illness bringing uncontrolled outbursts of kindness, patience, generosity and gentleness? I never have! Good things don't come from mental illness because good things don't come from spiritual pathogens.

Spiritual pathogens are sentient meaning they have awareness of their surroundings, who and what they are, and can think for themselves. They have emotions and intelligence. What they lack are physical bodies which is why they seek to inhabit a human body through which they can express their wickedness.

The expression of that wickedness is distinctly different from our own. This is because that behaviour is not our own but that of the spiritual pathogens. When the pathogens are removed, the true nature of that soul returns, and they are healed.

Some souls can audibly hear spiritual pathogens in their head. It is called psychosis. Medical science deems psychosis to be a loss of contact with reality. The sufferer is delusional or hallucinating. I beg to differ.

The voices are real. They can be heard and are coming from someone, somewhere. They are the voices of the spiritual entities attacking that human spirit. Let me prove this.

The voices a psychotic hears are intelligent, aware, motivated and destructive. There is nothing unreal about them especially if they lead someone to self-harm, harm others or commit suicide.

Often psychotic voices tell the sufferer to do dreadful things either to themselves or to others. These voices have power and authority over a sufferer's mind. That power and authority is spiritual power, it is spiritual warfare and is a reality.

The voices often terrify the sufferer which undermines the idea that the voices are coming from within the sufferer. How can someone speak to themselves coherently and at the same time bring terror to themselves forcing them to do things they don't want to do? They can't for that makes no sense The voices must belong to an entity outside of us.

How can someone speak to themselves and at the same time have absolutely no control over what they are saying? That just doesn't make sense either. How can someone be so frightened of the voices in their head that they do things they know are wrong but are too frightened to disobey? Those voices are coming from somewhere else beyond the sufferer. Something else has taken control. These are the pathogens, the spiritual entities behind mental illness.

Medical science does not recognise spiritual pathogens so have no idea where the voices are coming from or who is speaking to them. To believe the voices are coming from within the sufferer when the sufferer is terrified of them and has no control over them makes no sense.

Spiritual pathogens are entities, dark forces, that exist in the spiritual realm. For thousands of years, they were known to humankind as demons. Their nature was understood, and they were dealt with effectively through the spirit.

Today we have lost all understanding of these dark forces and turn to pharmaceuticals for healing. Medication is no match for demonic forces behind mental illness.

Science ridicules the idea of demons, considering them nothing more than figments of the imagination and are most definitely considered anti-science. If demons are anti-science how can they possibly exist? If they don't exist then where do the voices a psychotic hears come from? If demons don't exist then what are the forces behind mental illness?

How is it those forces can be overcome and healing happens when we apply spiritual warfare? There is far too much evidence proving demons do exist for medical science to just say, they can't exist because we think they are anti-science.

The reality of demons is lost today but that does not mean they have gone away. They haven't for they are still here. Demons are as real as is the mental illness they bring. They do exist and the Dead Sea Scrolls reveal to us who and what they are and how to overcome them. This is what I teach.

Those who struggle with mental illness know how powerful the spiritual forces behind mental illness can be. They know demons exist. Demonic forces are not anti-science, but spiritual science.

Demons operate outside the laws of physics, chemistry and biology because they are not physical, chemical or biological, but they are subject to the laws of spiritual science because they are spirit in form.

A human spirit with the Ruach ha Kodesh dwelling within it has power and authority over demons. We exert our authority over demons using spiritual warfare, which is the art of applying the laws of spiritual science. The art of spiritual warfare is taught in the Dead Sea Scrolls and here in this book.

I will teach you how to fight back against unseen forces behind mental illness. Let us start preparing for this battle by looking in the Dead Sea Scrolls.

THE DEAD SEA SCROLLS

Fig. 5

A SCROLL

A scroll is a strip of paper, papyrus or leather that is written upon, and rolled up for easy storage or carrying. It is read by rolling the scroll open from one end to the other. The Dead Sea Scrolls are a collection of ancient writings discovered in caves around the Dead Sea in 1947 by a 15yr old shepherd boy called Mohammed Dhib.

The scrolls themselves were over two thousand years old but the texts written upon them date back far earlier. Some of the writings are over six thousand years old, and are from the scroll of Enoch, purported to be the first book ever written. The original scroll of Enoch no longer survives but what he wrote has survived. It has been faithfully copied by scribes for the past six thousand years.

It is available on Amazon in English under the search term, 'Book of Enoch.' Our favoured edition is suggested in the reading list at the back of this book.

The scroll of Enoch was co-authored by the Angel of the Presence. Enoch reveals that the seven Archangels stand in the presence of the Creator, hence the term Angel of the Presence. Each Archangel has a specific function and responsibility within creation in both the spiritual realm and the earthly realm.

Archangel Uriel.
Uriel watches over the world and the underworld. He guides souls into the underworld, Sheol, where we rest in peace awaiting judgement. Uriel and his team manage all the moving parts on earth. Let me give you an example.

All the rivers of the world continually pour themselves into the sea, yet the sea does not rise, nor rivers run dry. This perpetual balance of forces and vast moving parts is not left to its own devices but overseen by Archangel Uriel and his team of angelic beings.

Archangel Raphael.
He is one of the holy angels who watch over the spirits of men.

Archangel Raguel.
He takes vengeance on the world of the luminaries, fallen angels, in the spiritual realm.

Archangel Michael.
He watches over the best part of mankind and over chaos.

Archangel Saraqael.
He is set over the spirits, who sin in the spirit.

Archangel Gabriel.
He is over the heavenly Paradise, and the Serpents and the Cherubim, strange and ferocious spiritual entities.

Archangel Remiel.
He is whom the Creator has set over those who rise, those who receive eternal life.

For two thousand years, this ancient library of scrolls was hidden in caves around Betharabba. Its discovery in 1947 is arguably one of the greatest archaeological discoveries ever, yet almost no one knows of it.

The scrolls document the inter-dimensional relationship between the Creator and humankind. They document eye-witness accounts from those who witnessed these extra-terrestrial encounters. The scrolls record several thousand years of human interaction between this world and the spiritual realm.

Fig. 6

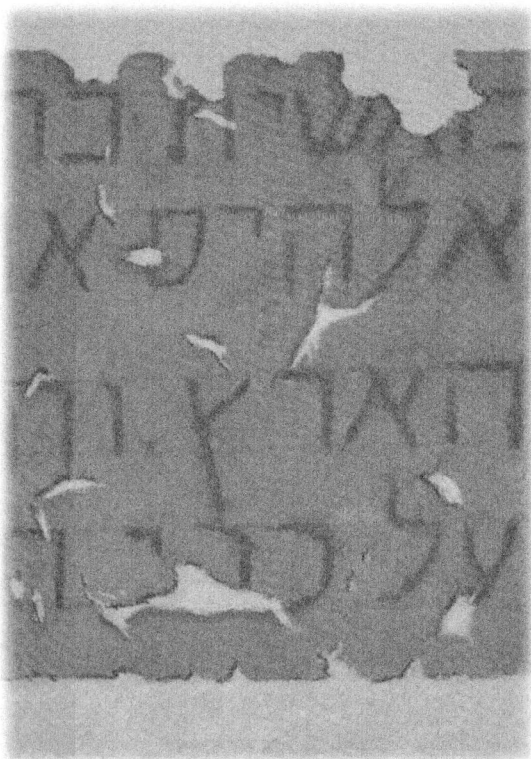

SCROLL FRAGMENT

These accounts are not mythical, allegorical or speculative, but written by those who saw what happened with their own eyes. The authors lived in different centuries, speaking different languages and living in different countries. This collection of scrolls could not have been curated by humankind because it spans thousands of years, different countries and cultures. Its curation itself is supernatural.

Fig. 7

SCROLL JARS HIDDEN IN CAVES
OF BETHARABBA

It would be almost impossible for a scholar to add to these scrolls anything meaningful without contradiction or error. The scrolls are meant as a gift to all humankind from the Creator. They are not a gift to the religious.

They are unique for they reveal the Creator's laws that enable us to thrive. They reveal the purpose of humankind and the ultimate gift of eternal life. No other documents on earth can compare to the Dead Sea Scrolls.

Claiming to be the Creator's own words and laws is a staggering claim, so how can we tell if this claim is credible? How can we be sure they are not a hoax? Let us put them to the test.

Firstly, no man could curate a complete library of scrolls revealing the Creator with over forty authors revealing parts of the same puzzle, spanning two thousand years, speaking different languages and without a single contradiction. That in itself is pretty amazing but does not prove their credibility. if we are going to use the scrolls in spiritual warfare they need to be thoroughly tested. So, how do we test them?

It is easier to test them than you might think. There are hundreds of prophecies within them foretelling the future. They reveal history in advance. Because they were written thousands of years ago, we have a lot of history from when they were written until now that we could look back on to see if they came true. If they didn't, then the scrolls are a hoax. If they did, then they are credible.

The Creator gives us prophecies no man could know. He makes Himself known by showing us things that are impossible to explain yet still exist. Prophecies accurately foretelling the future thousands of years in advance are impossible to explain yet exist in the scrolls. This is how the Creator makes Himself known.

If the prophecies we are going to test came true then that suggests history was planned by someone or something, from the start. Telling us what is going to happen in advance not only reassures us that there is a

Creator but that He wants us to know what is going to happen in advance so we will not fear what we see.

Being able to manage the future means creation is being managed. If it were not so, then how is it the prophecies are coming true? Who is managing creation? We are told it is being managed by millions of angelic beings. That is what they do. That is why they are there. They oversee planet earth and all the life that is on it.

The scrolls remind us we are mere mortals, not all-powerful, nor all-knowing, and that creation does not belong to us, nor are we in charge nor are we alone. We were given dominion over the animals and the plants and we have trashed it. We have behaved like spoilt children left alone in a sweet shop. Never have we been given the codes to creation, nor the ability or the brains to run it, thank goodness.

We do not have dominion over the sun, the moon the stars, nor over the tides of the sea nor the seasons of the year. We do not control the weather, nor the hours of the day, nor light nor dark. We do not have dominion over creation itself, but we are a much-loved part of a far bigger picture.

Nothing in creation, especially humankind, has been left to its own devices. Creation is far too precious for the Creator to leave to chance or for humankind to manage. What could possibly go wrong with men and women in charge I hear you say!

Creation is managed by millions of powerful angelic entities keeping all the moving parts working together and in their place according to a strict timetable. How do we know history is managed to a strict timetable?

Many of the prophecies are said to happen at specific moments in history. For this to be so, history must be managed to a strict timetable or it would not work. Let me show you.

In the scroll of Daniel a prophecy says,

"How long will it take for the vision to be fulfilled—that causes desolation, and the trampling underfoot of the LORD's people?" He said to me, "It will take 2,300 evenings and mornings. then the sanctuary will be reconsecrated."

Prophecies cannot be explained by science so are we to dismiss them even when we see them coming true? How can prophecies come true time and time again and yet be dismissed because they are anti-science. It is science who has a credibility problem, not the Dead Sea Scrolls. Angelic beings are also deemed anti-science, just like the prophecies, and are also dismissed by science despite irrefutable evidence proving their existence.

The scrolls reveal how the spiritual realm is divided into two territories. There is a heavenly kingdom and a satanic principality. Heavenly life forms are angelic and positive spiritual energy, satanic life forms are demonic and negative spiritual energy. We are spiritual beings inhabiting physical bodies so are affected by spiritual forces from the heavenly and satanic realms.

Threats to humankind exist in the Satanic and demonic realms. Spiritual attacks from the powers of darkness manifest primarily as mental illness. We can protect ourselves from spiritual attack by sheltering under the laws of life.

Applying these laws with skill is spiritual warfare. Spiritual forces are in conflict around us all the time whether we know it or not. The choice is, do we want to take control of those forces and fight back, or not?

The Dead Sea Scrolls clarify how the ten commandments can be used as a spiritual weapon, known as the sword of the spirit, against demons of mental illness. Demons know the ten commandments give us power ority over them, so will do all they can to prevent us from keeping .u be forewarned to be forearmed.

The Scrolls shed light on the mystery of death so we may not fear it. It explains the judgement of our souls on the last day so we can use our life to prepare for it. The scrolls are full of wisdom so we can life abundant, joyous and peaceful lives.

Around two thousand years ago these scrolls were sealed in earthenware jars and hidden in caves around Betharabba, (modern Qumran). Betharabba is to the north of the Dead Sea, from where the scrolls derive their name. Who put them there, and why?

The scrolls were placed in the caves by Aaronic priests who had once served in the temple in Jerusalem. The Aaronic priests were driven out in 165 BC by Pharisee Jews, who then took over the temple in Jerusalem.

Pharisee Jews are not a Biblical people as they claim. They are not from the tribe of Judah as many believe. They are not even Hebrew but Persian, hence the term Pharisee which comes from the word Farsi, the name of the Persian language. This was prophesied in the scroll of Revelation written two thousand years ago which says,

Behold, I will make them of the synagogue of Satan, who say they are Jews (from the tribe of Judah) and are not but do lie!

The Pharisee religion still exists today, as Rabbinic Judaism. Pharisee Jews oversaw the temple in Jerusalem in the days of the Messiah. It was the Pharisees who falsely accused Him of blasphemy, had Him flogged and then had Him crucified. To this day they still despise the Messiah.

Rabbinic Judaism has nothing to do with the Creator or the Messiah, nor are they a Biblical people, nor are they even Hebrew, but they are religious. Is it any wonder we are warned to stay away from them.

The religious Pharisees drove the 'Aaronic Priests' out of the temple in Jerusalem and into the wilderness of Betharabba near the Dead Sea.

There the Aaronic priests settled, keeping knowledge of the Creator alive and protecting the scrolls.

John the Baptist lived and worked there and even baptised the Messiah near their wilderness settlement. John the Baptist descended directly from Aaron, older brother of Moses, on his mother's side which qualified him to be an Aaronic High Priest. He and the Messiah were also cousins.

They certainly were not Pharisees for the Messiah had many harsh words for the religious of His day. Their reign of wickedness ended in 70AD when the temple was brought to ruins at the hands of the Roman empire. Not one stone stands upon another yet their religion known today as Rabbinic Judaism continues to flourish.

Fig.8

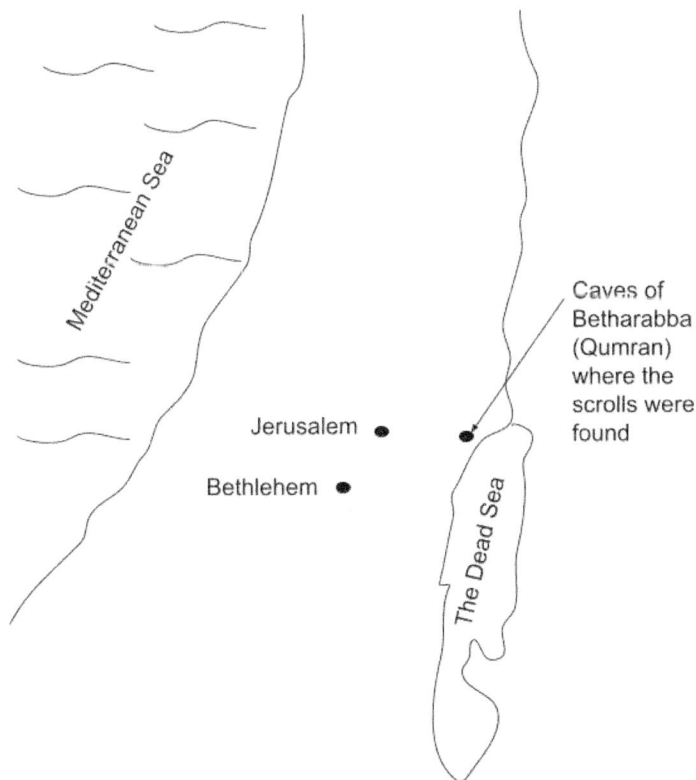

Map to the caves of Betharabba

Foreseeing the destruction by the Roman empire, the Aaronic priests hid the priceless scrolls in caves around their settlement. There they lay undisturbed for two thousand years until they were found in 1947.

These scrolls are the original scrolls of the Old Testament Bible and the Jewish Torah, though both have been mercilessly edited by religion, rendering them spiritually powerless. The scrolls remained unchanged and are what I share with you now.

Who are the Aaronic priests? Aaron, from where the term 'Aaronic' comes, was the older brother of Moses. Moses wrote some of the Dead Sea Scrolls including the scroll of Jubilees which we will be testing later.

Aaron helped his brother Moses lead the Hebrews out of Egypt and was appointed by the Creator to be guardian of the scrolls. Direct descendants of Aaron became the priests who guarded the scrolls, hence the term, Aaronic priests. John the Baptist was a direct descendent of Aaron so had the birth right to be an Aaronic High Priest.

Jews today accuse those who oppose them of antisemitism. This is wrong for they have no right to say this! They are not a semitic people so cannot claim antisemitism. Let me explain.

The term Semitic comes from Shem, Noah's first-born son and great, great grandson of Enoch, whose scroll we will test later. Hebrews are semitic because they came from Shem's bloodline. That is what makes us semitic.

Jews today are not Hebrew but Ashkenazi. Ashkenaz was the grandson of Japheth, Noah's third son. How can they claim antisemitism when they are not even semitic, or even Hebrew. Maybe they should start claiming anti-Ashkenaz instead. It would be more honest.

It is plain to see from the few things I have shared already from the Dead Sea Scrolls how several authorities would have a lot of explaining to do if the truth was to be made widely known.

THE
ORIGIN OF DEMONS

Do not fear the term Demons. Their reality is very different from the demons portrayed in movies. Demons are not as dramatic or obvious as Hollywood, art and literature would have us believe.

They are far more subtle and devious relying on stealth in their deception. Because they operate unseen in the darkness causing chaos from the shadows very few people believe they exist. Our ignorance is very much to their advantage.

The Creator's spirit, the Ruach ha Kodesh, gives us spiritual power and authority over demons. Without the Ruach ha Kodesh we do not have the power nor the authority to fend them off. The Ruach ha Kodesh enters our spirit when we keep the ten commandments. This is their power.

Disbelief in demons allows them to wreak havoc with impunity, for who blames an enemy no one believes exists. Disbelief in demons suits demons. The more they are considered a figment of the imagination the more freedom they have to cause harm and suffering at will.

They are no more a figment of the imagination than the mental illness or chronic sickness they bring. Those who experience mental illness know how powerful those forces are. Demons cause the human soul a great deal of harm and suffering.

If we don't believe demons exists, then we can't fight them. Disbelief renders a soul defenceless to demonic attack for the first law of spiritual warfare is to know your enemy. If we don't believe the enemy exists, then we will continue to know nothing about them. One nil to the demons!

The origin of demons is fascinating and extraordinary. What I am going to tell you may sound implausible at first but stay with me and I will prove it to be true. The truth will astound you. I have evidence from several sources that I will share with you now.

When I started my research into demonic warfare over forty-five years ago, I was sceptical of demons. My preconceived ideas were upended as I followed the evidence. I followed the laws of spiritual science and came to the truth which in this instance, really is stranger than fiction. So, let me share with you what I know to be true.

The origin of demons begins with the angelic beings that manage the many moving parts of planet earth. These angelic beings are called 'Watchers.' There are millions of them overseeing the seasons, the weather, the tides, the rivers and the seas, our solar system and all the other moving parts within creation.

They are currently managing the warming of the planet that will result in climate change disasters prophesied in the book of Revelation. These disasters are prophesied to happen in the last days which we are entering now.

Humankind, governments and activists with their green agenda will make no difference to what is prophesied. Our efforts are too little, too late, for we are entering the days of those prophecies now.

There will be periods of intense heat, diseases and plagues, droughts, famines, mass migrations, earthquakes, great storms, tsunamis and volcanic eruptions, wars and rumours of wars. All these things were prophesied two thousand years ago and mocked by science and academia, who have no answers as to what to do in the face of these impending disasters.

The point is that earth is managed by angelic beings called Watchers. Six thousand years ago two hundred of these 'Watcher Angels' deserted their heavenly posts and fell to earth on Mount Hermon in the middle east.

Their intention was to procreate with human women. They did. Their offspring were neither angelic nor human. They were hybrid humans who were not a part of creation nor did they belong in it.

When these hybrid human creatures died, their spirits had nowhere to go. They had no place in creation, they had no destiny. They became trapped in the spiritual realm, the same spiritual realm we are connected to. These unclean, unnatural spirits became the demonic entities behind mental illness. Let me show you.

Fig.9

MOUNT HERMON

Whilst overseeing earth, Watchers were beguiled by human women. They lusted after them. Angels are spirit beings in the male form who are eternal, so there is no such thing as, or need of, women or procreation in the heavenly realm.

Procreation has no meaning or purpose in the heavenly realm so when they saw women and their role in procreation, they were mesmerised and enthralled. They were filled with lust and fascination because no such thing existed in the heavenly realm.

Their lust drove them to fall from heaven, deserting their heavenly posts to procreate with human women so they may have families of their own, on earth. They had never seen such a thing in the heavenly realm and desired it greatly for themselves.

A cohort of two hundred Watcher angels made a covenant among themselves and swore on oath agreeing they would all jointly be held accountable, should they be judged for what they were about to do.

Watcher angels knew the laws of procreation, which state each is to procreate according to its kind. They knew that what they were doing was a gross violation of the law of procreation.

The angels fell to earth, on to Mount Hermon in Israel, under the leadership of a powerful angel called Semjaza. In Hebrew 'Hermon' means to make accursed or to consecrate, devote or forfeit. Even the etymology (historical origin) of the name of Mount Hermon references this extraordinary extra-terrestrial event.

The etymology of ancient place names often reveals historical events. Mount Hermon is an example of a place name preserving an extra-terrestrial encounter between this realm and the spiritual realm.

Fig.10

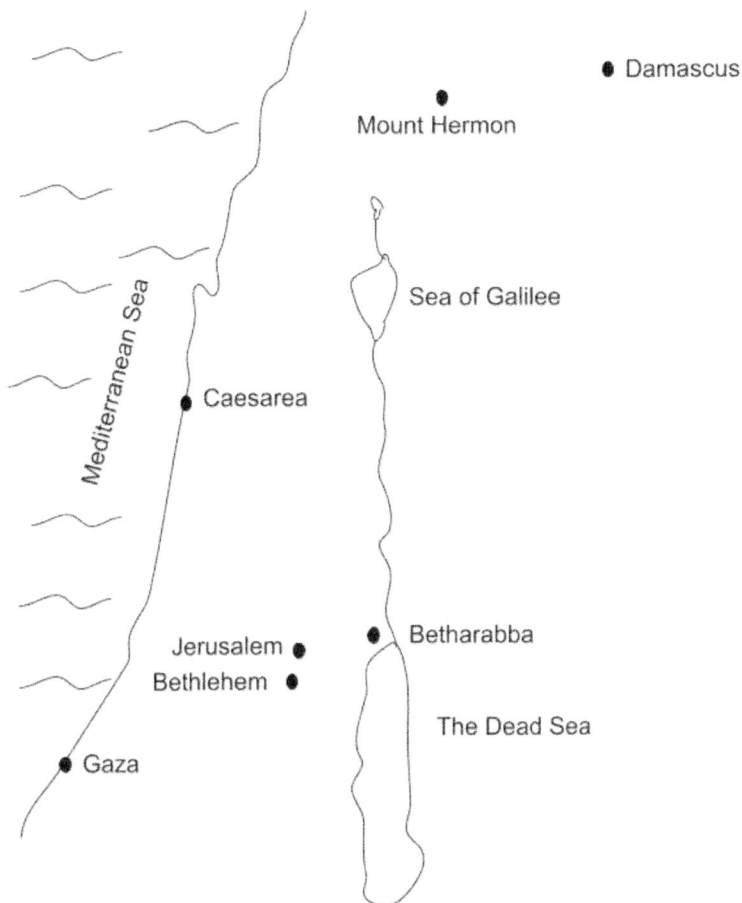

MAP OF MOUNT HERMON

The ancient mythologies of many cultures tell of alien beings coming from the stars and living among them. Egyptian to South American, African to European. Many cultures describe beings that came from the stars and ruled over them, demanding obedience, tribute and sacrifice. This form of rule by the fallen angels became a template for the practice of religion. Religion does not come from the Dead Sea Scrolls but from the vile practices of the fallen angels.

Fallen angels took human women and procreated with them. Their offspring were neither human nor angelic but unnatural hybrid humans. They were a violation of the laws of procreation which state,

'Each was created according to its kind, male and female they were made, so they may procreate according to their kind.'

The offspring of this unnatural union were called *Nephilim* which in Hebrew means 'fallen ones.' The Hebrew word 'naphal' is to fall'. They were hybrid humans, and they were giants.

They had superior knowledge, capabilities, size and strength and were continually evil in nature. There was no kindness or humanity in them for they were not fully human nor fully angelic. They lusted continuously for bloodshed, and cruelty, including cannibalism, even of their own.

The exploits of the gods in Greek mythology are reflective of the behaviour and nature of the Nephilim offspring of the fallen Watcher Angels. These gods came from the sky, having angelic powers, great strength and superior knowledge.

In Greek mythology it tells of how they procreated with human women and the strange creatures they produced. Many of the mythologies around the world tell of similar beings behaving in similar ways.

Titans, Cyclops and Ogres are hybrid humans Their evil, violent, and cannibalistic nature is mirrored in the Dead Sea Scrolls account of the Nephilim. There are parallels in mythologies around the world from India to North America that are so similar and numerous they cannot be mere coincidence, nor can they be ignored.

When archaeology became popular in the 1800s many giant skeletal remains up to twenty-five feet tall were unearthed. They were once in museums for us all to see until the early 1900s. Where are they now?

The theories of evolution proposed in the1850's by Charles Darwin and adopted by mainstream science, could not account for these giant skeletons. The Dead Sea Scrolls, the Torah and the Bible had many accounts of giants with great strength including Nimrod, Goliath of Gath, and Og of Bashan. This gave mainstream science a big problem.

Science claims life evolved. Giant skeletons cannot be explained by evolution. The world of science decided that the answer to their problem was to destroy all the evidence that disagreed with them, so that is what they did.

From the early 1900s the Smithsonian Institute, on behalf of mainstream science removed and destroyed from museums across the world all skeletal evidence of giants, to protect the precious doctrines of evolution.

Even today the Smithsonian Institute denies the existence of giant skeletal remains proving the existence of the Nephilim. Thanks to the internet there are many Victorian periodicals published online so we can read the articles that were written by archaeologists and the giant skeletons they unearthed back in the 1800s.

The Dead Sea Scrolls undermine the theories of evolution which is why science and academia mock them. The Smithsonian Institute's loyalties lay with mainstream science and evolution, and not with the truth.

Despite their efforts to destroy the truth, evidence of the Nephilim remains. The remnant of this interbreeding between angelic beings and human women is found in the skeletal remains of Neanderthal man. There are many parallels between the Nephilim and Neanderthal man I will share with you shortly.

Giant skeletons have been unearthed all over the world, even in the UK. The pantomime, Jack and the Beanstalk was originally called 'Jack and the Giant Killer,' and is part of Cornish folklore. The refrain sung by the giant called Blunderbore in the pantomime story goes:

Fee fi fo fum, I smell the blood of an Englishman. Be he alive, be he dead, I shall grind his bones to make my bread.

Nephilim giants lived around the world, including England. Who imagined the likeable cartoon character Shrek, was rooted in the Nephilim, the hybrid human offspring of the fallen angels?

Giants have been documented through history such as Nimrod the great hunter who killed lions with his bare hands and the giant Goliath, and his brothers. They are Nephilim bloodlines.

The Nephilim king, Og of Bashan, whose existence is not disputed, was known to have a 13-foot-long iron bed. From Norse gods to Egyptian gods, from South American gods to African and Indian gods, they all tell of hybrid humans with god-like abilities ruling over them.

The Nephilim were a corruption of human DNA. Echoes of this corruption are seen in the remains of Neanderthal man. By accepting the existence of Neanderthal man, mainstream science has tacitly, and unknowingly accepted Nephilim giants as documented in the Dead Sea Scrolls. There is no other explanation for the existence of Neanderthal man.

Is there a connection between Neanderthal man and Watcher fallen angels? Let me show you, because this is fascinating!

Scientific data confirms Neanderthals did not contribute any mitochondrial DNA to the human gene pool. Mitochondrial DNA is passed only from a mother to a daughter. Neanderthal man has no mitochondrial DNA. This suggests that they were only male. 'Watcher Angels' were also only male and only had sons.

The absence of a female is only possible if there is no mitochondrial DNA passed from one generation to the next. This is seen in Neanderthals. Evidence suggests there were no Neanderthal women because there is no mitochondrial DNA. Fallen angels were also only male in form so would not have had any mitochondrial DNA to contribute to the gene pool to start with.

Mainstream science suggests Neanderthal man originated in the middle-east and spread outwards from there. Mount Hermon where the Watcher

Angels first fell, is in the middle of the middle east. Another parallel that cannot be ignored.

Neanderthals were not Homosapien, but part Homosapien and part angelic. They were not fully human but hybrids, sharing humanoid characteristics. They were a different race of human beings, but not human beings. So, where did the Neanderthals come from? The only plausible explanation is the falling of the Watcher Angels recorded in the Dead Sea Scrolls.

Today around 2% of Neanderthal DNA is present in modern humans. It must have come from somewhere. The parallels between the Nephilim, offspring of the fallen angels, and Neanderthal man, are too numerous and significant for us to ignore.

Science has no answers as to where Neanderthal man came from, and evolution can't explain them. The Dead Sea Scrolls reveal precisely what happened, yet scientists disregard the Dead Sea Scrolls as irrelevant without investigation. You would think curiosity would get the better of them. Sadly not, but it did me!

What does this have to do with overcoming mental illness? The offspring of the fallen angels were giants called Nephilim. They were not part of creation, nor did they belong to the Creator. They have no place in His creation.

When the Nephilim giants died, their spirits had nowhere to go. Unlike human or animal spirits, they had no destiny within them. They were not part of creation so there was no plan for their spirits to rest in Sheol, the underworld. They had nowhere to go after their bodies died.

Their spirits became trapped in the spiritual realm. These spirits are wicked and evil by nature and seek to cause harm wherever they go. Because we are also spirit, our world overlaps theirs as theirs overlaps ours.

We are subject to spiritual forces which means we are exposed to these malevolent spirits. These unclean disembodied spirits of the Nephilim giants are the unseen spiritual forces behind mental illness. They are the demons of mental illness.

The scroll of Jubilees tells us that ninety per cent of these evil spirits were cast by the Creator into the great Abyss of Condemnation, deep within the earth, for the sake of humankind. The fallen Watcher Angels have also been cast into the great Abyss awaiting their judgement.

Widespread corruption of the human DNA by Watcher angels procreating with human women was the reason for the great flood in the days of Noah. It is written that there were giants on the earth at that time and after the flood.

This suggests some Nephilim may have survived the great flood. That would account for the continued existence of Neanderthal man and the two per cent of Neanderthal DNA found in Asian and European gene pools today.

I am convinced through decades of research, that the demons behind mental illness are the disembodied spirits of the Nephilim. They are malevolent spiritual entities trapped in the spiritual realm. Because we are spirit, we too are connected to that realm. Our connection gives them access to our spirit if we allow them.

Demonic spirits of the Nephilim are the unseen forces that lay behind self-harming, suicide, anxiety, fear, depression, psychosis, addiction, obsession, compulsion, jealousy and murder. The malevolent forces behind mental illness that seize control of the mind, are the disembodied spirits of the Nephilim who once lived on earth.

Because we have lost all knowledge of them, we do not see them or understand the chaos and suffering they cause. We cannot fight what we do not know so demons continue to attack us with impunity. We have no protection because we have no concept of the threat. As was written in the scrolls, my people perish through lack of knowledge.

Many today perish through mental illness and chronic sickness. When we look at the facts about mental illness we can see evidence of these spiritual forces. Firstly, we lose control of our mental faculties. Who or what seizes control from us?

Something sentient and intelligent must seize control for the mind does not grind to a halt but is driven into dark, destructive places. That is the nature of mental illness. The destructive nature of mental illness that takes over when we lose control is proof of spiritual forces in our mind that do not belong to us.

Where do the voices heard by psychotics come from? They must be coming from somewhere. The sufferer is often terrified of the voices that force them to do what they know is wrong. They are powerless to fight back. That is also evidence of demonic forces seizing control.

If demonic forces do not exist, how is it spiritual warfare works? What is it the sword of the spirit overcomes and brings healing, if it is not demonic forces.

How is it the 10 commandments lead to countless healings? If demons don't exist, how is healing through the spirit even possible? It is because demonic forces are in the spirit, pharmaceutical medications do not work. There is no pharmaceutical medication that can cure mental illness because mental illness is in the spirit, not the body.

Those who do not believe demons exist, must believe the Dead Sea Scrolls are wrong in what they say. That means the Bible is wrong, as is the Torah. Moses is wrong, and the Creator is also wrong. The Messiah who was crucified for what He believed is wrong, Abraham, Isaiah, Jeremiah, Ezra and Ezekiel are all wrong, and the twelve disciples were also wrong.

They are all wrong, but apparently someone who does not believe demons exist is right. If I were that outnumbered I would certainly stop and have a re-think.

THE PRINCIPLES OF
SPIRITUAL WARFARE

Spiritual warfare is happening all around us affecting every area of our lives. Positive spiritual forces are constantly in conflict with negative forces. Losing contact with our spirit means we are no longer aware of the flow of these spiritual forces around us.

All we see are the outcomes of this conflict such as coincidences, unexpected opportunities, misfortune or sudden surprises, both good and bad. Most know nothing of the unseen forces operating behind life's outcomes.

Those who are wise in the spirit have intuition, empathy, insight and foresight so they can see how these forces are playing out. Understanding how the flow of these spiritual forces work around us means we can take control of them and use them to our advantage. Life becomes easier.

Controlling spiritual forces around us is spiritual warfare. We can influence the circumstances around us, seize opportunities, avoid calamities and stack the odds of success in our favour.

Spiritual warfare is not wishful thinking. It is strategic, targeted, intelligent and highly effective. It is somewhere between mixed martial arts of the mind and a courtroom battle.

Spiritual warfare is not about wills or brute strength. At its simplest, it is a legal argument. If demons have no lawful right to be here, we can lawfully evict them.

Spiritual warfare is not subjective. It does not involve emotions, opinions, brute strength, bias or ideas of what is fair or what is not, any more than a court of law would. It is about what is lawful. Spiritual warfare is a legal battle fought using spiritual laws.

Demons have a lawful right to possess and torment any human soul that chooses to live lawlessly. If a life is lived outside the laws of the ten commandments then that life is fair game for demons, according to the laws.

A lawless soul lives in negative territory. Negative territory belongs to Satan, the Prince of this World, and his demons. It is their territory so they have every right to be there. We cannot live in their territory and expect to be protected from them.

Keeping the commandments brings the human soul into positive, lawful territory where it is protected from demons, for they cannot go there.

Bringing a human soul from negative territory into positive territory is how we remove a demon's lawful right to torment that soul. This is how we evict the demons behind mental illness, otherwise they will remain, for the soul is remaining in their territory.

When a mental illness is seen to be incurable, recurrent, chronic or persistent it is because the soul it inhabits is in lawless territory. Only when the soul enters positive lawful territory does the mental illness go for it cannot exist in positive territory. This is a basic principle of spiritual warfare.

The ten commandments are the foundation to the spiritual laws of life. There are many more spiritual laws covering every aspect of life. They come in parables, proverbs, psalms, and proclamations. They empower the spirit.

There is a lifetime of knowledge and wisdom to explore as you delve into the world of spiritual health.. They are the spiritual laws of life. Demons are subject to spiritual laws so the more we know the greater the power and authority we have over them.

It matters not whether a person is Christian, Hindu, Muslim, Jewish, Buddhist, Sikh or irreligious, for there is nothing stopping them embracing the commandments of their true Creator for He made all of us!

A Buddhist has the same creator as a Hindu, a Muslim, a Jew, a Christian, a Hebrew, or a non-believer. We all have the same Creator. Religion may separate us, but spiritual health and the Dead Sea Scrolls bring us back together.

Those who believe their religious faith will protect them spiritually are misled because religion and malevolent spiritual forces are on the same side. One cannot offer protection from the other for they both belong to the same spiritual principality, or kingdom. A kingdom or principality divided cannot stand. We cannot drive out lawless energy using the same lawless energy. It won't work.

Religion is a worldly power and worldly power belongs to the Prince of this World, who is called Satan. The demons behind mental illness also belong to Satan. Religion, Satan and demons are spiritually all on the same side. This is why the Creator does not work through religion, Satan or demons.

The power needed to evict demons that lurk behind mental illness must come from outside the satanic and demonic realm. It must come from positive territory; it must be positive energy if it is to overcome negative energy and that only comes from the Creator.

We either believe in the Creator or we do not. No one can say they might believe, or they think they do. No one can only half believe. We cannot sit on the fence when it comes to belief because there is no fence!

Belief is not ambivalent for ambivalence is disbelief. Disbelief is the territory of Satan. We either believe in a Creator which is positive territory, or we do not which is negative territory. There is no third territory. The Creator tells us,

> 'He who is with me is for me,
> he who is not with me is against me.'

No one Is let off the hook when it comes to belief in the Creator because no one is let off the hood when it comes to the judgement of the soul on the last day. Belief comes from knowledge. Many do not believe in the Creator because they do not know anything of the Creator. We cannot believe in something we know nothing about. The knowledge we need is in the scrolls of Enoch, Jubilees and the Bible. The Bible cannot be understood without the scrolls of Enoch and Jubilees. That is why we will test all three later in the book.

Generations of souls have been robbed by mainstream science and academia of the knowledge that would have given them belief in the Creator. Entire generations have been left without any spiritual truth in which to believe. With disbelief we can do nothing.

The truth that was denied them is that the spirit of the Creator can dwell in any human soul if invited. When He does, the spiritual DNA of that soul is changed and becomes a new creature, spiritually. We become spiritually connected, empowered and marked as belonging to the Creator. It is the biggest transformation that can happen in the earthly life of a soul.

A soul is like a smart device. Smart devices without internet are not that smart. The moment a smart device connects to the internet is becomes very smart. So it is when a soul connects to the Creator, it becomes fully alive and supernaturally smart. A soul with the Creator's spirit dwelling within it is unstoppable.

Belief connects us to the Creator. Belief starts with the ten commandments. It is declared in the very first commandment. That is how important belief is.

Beliefs grow. Deep rooted beliefs have limitless power and can withstand great adversity. Shallow beliefs are easily uprooted. Spiritual health is dependent on belief. The deeper rooted the belief the stronger the health of the spirit.

Over a lifetime of learning the spirit can grow very deep roots, produce a lot of fruit and even transform the physical world around us. This spiritual ability has been known as mind over matter for the mind is spirit and matter is the physical world around us.

Eternal life is the prize for those who have deeply held beliefs in the truth. It is written that the power of belief can move mountains. The point being belief matters. It is the key!

Beliefs have immense power whether they are positive or negative. Negative beliefs can bring about negative outcomes as positive beliefs can bring about positive outcomes.

Whether you believe you can or you believe you can't,

either way you will most probably be right.

Most hold beliefs that have never been tested. Most beliefs are not even true, for example, most Christians believe Jesus was the name of the Messiah and His birthday was on the 25th of December. None of that is true yet a commonly held belief.

We need to constantly check the quality and truth of our beliefs. Test everything! When I started to test my beliefs, I discovered almost everything I had been told was untrue. The first belief we need to secure is belief in the Creator, however He appears to you. This is not religion so if your vision of the Creator is different from mine, that's OK.

As our belief in the Creator grows and becomes deep rooted, we become incredibly resilient to mental illness. Belief in the Creator is the opposite of mental illness, for one is positive and one is negative. They cannot both exist at the same time. Belief in the Creator promises us a spirit of courage and of a sound mind. For it is written in the second scroll of Timothy that,

The Creator, Yahuah Elohim, has not given us a spirit of fear, but of power and of love and of a sound mind.

Belief in the Creator transforms the quality of our thoughts. Our thoughts govern our emotions and behaviour. This is how belief in the Creator will steer us to a life of joy, peace and abundance.

It is written,

'I am exactly where
my thoughts have brought me.'

We can learn how to regulate the quality of our thoughts and beliefs and to check on them regularly. Positive beliefs bring good fortune and good health, whereas negative beliefs bring misfortune and poor health. Controlling positive and negative energy is the foundation to spiritual warfare.

Spiritual warfare weaponizes spiritual laws. We have an enemy we need to overcome. The first principle is to know your enemy. The second is to know yourself.

The enemy has existed for thousands of years so knows the spiritual laws far better than we do. We are mortal souls with short lives on earth so have far less time to learn and apply those laws. We cannot fight this enemy ourselves or in our own strength. The enemy has power and authority over us until we invite the Ruach ha Kodesh to dwell in our spirit. We then have power and authority over them. This is a principle of spiritual warfare.

To thrive in this life we need to know the spiritual laws of life for they give us the weapons of spiritual warfare.. They were given to us in the beginning. They give us spiritual health and protection. We cannot thrive without them.

HOW
WE LET DEMONS IN

Demons do not break into our mind or our spirit. We let them in. There are two ways we let demons in. The first is by breaking spiritual laws of life, the ten commandments. Even if we don't know we are breaking them, we give demons permission to harm us.

Breaking laws is the definition of lawlessness. A lawless life is unprotected from spiritual attack for it is to leave the door open.. Keeping those laws is how we place ourselves under their protection.

The second way we let demons in is by dwelling on thoughts that are negative. Negative thoughts are dark, carnal, and lawless. They take us into negative territory. We have no protection from negative forces when we live in negative territory. It is easy to drift into negative territory. Let me show you how easy it is to drift into negative territory, using jealousy as an example.

Jealous thoughts come easily to some and create dark, negative energy that attracts spiritual pathogens. They will feed off jealous energy making the situation worse. The jealous energy builds up until it becomes uncontrollable. It lakes on a life of its own. We cannot get rid of it; we think of nothing else; it makes us ill and our thoughts become very dark and unstable. This is when we know we have let the demons in

The ten commandments tell us specifically not to dwell on jealousy because it lets demons of jealousy in, and they are not easy to get rid of.

It is the same with adulterous thoughts, or thoughts of betrayal, stealing, murder or vengeance. They too can quickly spiral out of control. The commandments teach us how to discern the quality of our thoughts so we don't let demons in by accident. Life is much nicer if we can avoid them.

CHAPTER 4
THE 10 COMMANDMENTS

THE TEN COMMANDMENTS

The ten commandments are the spiritual laws of life. They have the spiritual and psychological power needed to transform lives. No life is beyond the reach of the ten commandments. This I will prove throughout the book.

The commandments are the bedrock to spiritual and mental health and the power behind spiritual warfare. It is not possible to heal the spirit without them. Because they have been largely forgotten our spiritual and mental health have declined dramatically. We are no longer resilient to spiritual attack and mental decline, nor can we remember how to self-heal.

The commandments are a contract. They are an agreement between humankind and the Creator with promises made on both sides. It is an eternal promise with no end. There is nothing else on earth like them.

The 10 commandments were written by the Creator. He wrote them Himself on tablets of stone four thousand years ago and gave them to Moses on Mount Sinai as a gift for humankind. To those who enter His covenant He promises the ultimate of all gifts, eternal life! This is what makes the ten commandments unlike anything else on earth. There is nothing on earth that can promise eternal life, except the ten commandments.

The tablets of stone inscribed with the covenant is somewhere on earth. They are in a golden treasure chest called, the Ark of the Covenant. which has a solid gold lid with two angels cast in solid gold on the top. In the 1980s, the Ark of the Covenant was dramatized in the film, Raiders of the Lost Ark with Harrison Ford as Indiana Jones who sets out to find the lost Ark of the Covenant.

This covenant was written four thousand years ago, for you! It is as pertinent now as it was on the day it was given to Moses. It is time to look at each of them one by one and then tease them apart to reveal their power.

THE TEN COMMANDMENTS

1st

I AM YAHUAH ELOHIM,
CREATOR OF HEAVEN AND EARTH.
YOU SHALL HAVE NO OTHER ELOHIM BEFORE ME.

2nd

YOU SHALL NOT MAKE FOR YOURSELF AN IMAGE IN THE
FORM OF ANYTHING IN HEAVEN ABOVE, OR ON EARTH
BENEATH, OR IN THE WATERS BELOW. YOU SHALL NOT
BOW DOWN TO THEM OR WORSHIP THEM.

3rd

YOU SHALL NOT MISUSE THE NAME OF YAHUAH ELOHIM.

4th

REMEMBER THE SABBATH DAY BY KEEPING IT HOLY. SIX
DAYS SHALL YOU LABOUR AND DO ALL YOUR WORK, BUT
THE SEVENTH DAY IS A SABBATH TO YAHUAH ELOHIM.
ON IT YOU SHALL DO NO WORK

FOR IN SIX DAYS YAHUAH ELOHIM MADE THE HEAVENS
AND THE EARTH, THE SEA AND ALL THAT IS IN THEM, BUT
HE RESTED ON THE SEVENTH DAY. THEREFORE, HE
BLESSED THE SABBATH DAY AND MADE IT HOLY.

*HONOUR YOUR FATHER AND MOTHER, SO THAT YOU
MAY LIVE LONG IN THE LAND YAHUAH ELOHIM
IS GIVING YOU*

6th

YOU SHALL NOT COMMIT MURDER

7th

YOU SHALL NOT COMMIT ADULTERY

8th

YOU SHALL NOT STEAL

9th

*YOU SHALL NOT GIVE FALSE TESTIMONY
AGAINST YOUR NEIGHBOUR.*

10th

*YOU SHALL NOT COVET YOUR NEIGHBOUR'S HOUSE. YOU
SHALL NOT COVET YOUR NEIGHBOUR'S WIFE, OR HIS
MALE OR FEMALE SERVANT, HIS OX OR DONKEY, OR
ANYTHING THAT BELONGS TO
YOUR NEIGHBOUR!*

These are the 10 commandments. Do not be misled by their apparent simplicity and brevity. They are far reaching and immensely powerful.

The judicial system of western culture was built on them. They have served us well for two thousand years. Modern lawmakers are now making laws that violate the commandments. We will not have to wait long to see the lawless outcomes of these violations. Know now that they will bring misfortune across the nation.

Our lawmakers have wandered so far into negative territory we now have 'none-crime hate incidents'. I do not see any none-crime hate incidents in the ten commandments for they do not make sense. There is only lawfulness and lawlessness. Laws are not regulated or set by our emotions; wouldn't you know!

We now have lawless lawmakers in the UK today, bringing spiritual misfortune on the nation. The spiritual protection our nation has enjoyed for generations is being lifted as we turn against the spiritual laws of life.

Law and order, poverty and health, as well as basic services like water and food are going to be in steep decline in the UK until spiritual lawfulness is reinstated over this nation. It is prophesied to get far worse because our leaders will not listen for they are blind guides and deaf to reason.

Those who keep the commandments will be protected. The Creator promises to care for us if we care for Him. We have angelic protection. The Creator cares for His own. They will be protected spiritually by Him from the prophecies in the days to come.

The commandments are spiritual laws. Laws have definable outcomes. The outcome to keeping them is definably positive whereas the outcome to breaking them is definably negative. Those outcomes are not luck or chance or accidental, but definable outcomes from definable laws.

Let us unlock them and see what is there.

UNLOCKING
THE TEN COMMANDMENTS

The ten commandments give us spiritual power and authority over demons, and demons know it. They will avoid souls empowered by the ten commandments seeking out low hanging fruit as in the unprotected souls. They can't bite back. This is how the ten commandments protects us from the powers of darkness in the spiritual realm.

Every soul will be judged on the last day. The commandments are the metric by which we will be judged. The quality of our life will be measured by the ten commandments. How do we know this?

Our lives will be judged according to lawfulness and lawlessness. The commandments define what is lawful and what is not. The scales of judgement weigh lawful energy against lawless energy. When the scales tip in favour of lawfulness the soul is judged well, whereas when the scales tip in favour of lawlessness they are judged poorly.

Knowing this changes everything for it enables us to prepare for the judgement of our soul. This is the purpose of our life on earth. The meaning of life on earth is the gift of eternal life given to those who are judged well. What is not to like?

No soul is spared from the judgement, not even the spirits of angels or demons. Denying the judgement will not absolve us from it. Those who are wise prepare for it. The foolish sadly perish by their lack of knowledge.

Those judged well are led to the narrow gate leading to eternal life. The ten commandments are the keys to that gate.

Those judged lawless are led to the broad gate of destruction for which no keys are necessary. Those souls are cast into the lake of eternal fire and will no longer exist. It is written there will be weeping, wailing, great sadness and gnashing of teeth on that day, for it will be too late to change anything.

Many will be shocked to discover that the Creator they mocked, and His scrolls they scoffed at, were indeed true. They rejected eternal life for what? Eternal death! This is probably the worse decision anyone can make in their life; it is certainly the most far reaching. Eternal life is not denied to anyone who chooses it. Sadly, few will.

Many will be shocked to discover their religion was not the path to the Creator or eternal life. The religious are warned in their scriptures many times not to be deceived. The promise of eternal life through religion is the great deceit the religious are endlessly warned about. Eternal life only comes from a relationship with the Creator, which is to do with spiritual health and which starts with the ten commandments, not religion.

The souls found wanting on the day of judgement are thrown into the lake of eternal fire and will exist no more, which sounds frightening and harsh, but the spiritual realm has made no secret of it. It is not the Creator's fault if science and academia mock Him, scoff at His judgement, and then lead millions of souls to their spiritual death by hiding the truth from them. How is that the fault of the Creator?

What science and academia have done over many generations is truly wicked. Bringing spiritual destruction upon themselves is one thing, leading millions of souls into spiritual destruction by using their willing ignorance to sow disbelief is another. They will account for what they have done, as will we all.

Surely it is better I tell you these things now so you can know the truth and prepare for it, than for you to find out when it is too late. Proverbs say,

Wisdom starts with fear of Yahuah Elohim.

Fearing the judgement is to be wise for fear of the judgement is the foundation of wisdom.

Many ask, why fear the Creator if He loves us? We are not to fear His love, we are to fear His judgement. Those who do not fear Him, or His judgement really are in spiritual trouble.

The foolish who choose science, academia and religion for their salvation are free to go their way, doing as they choose. We have all been given free will and not even the Creator, having given it in the first place will violate it.

When judgement comes, no one can say. they did not know, for they were told, but chose not to hear. Nor can they change their fate for it will be too late, for it was their choice!

I am not alone in speaking of these things nor am I making these things up. The Apostle Matthew confirms what I have been saying when he wrote.

"Enter through the narrow gate. For wide is the gate and broad is the road that leads to destruction, and many enter through it. But small is the gate and narrow the road that leads to life, and only a few find it."

The narrow gate leads to eternal life, the key being the ten commandments I am sharing with you now. The decision to keep them or not is entirely yours for no one will force you. You have the freedom to choose your eternal future. Your life is in your hands.

The ten commandments also have psychological power. Why, if they have psychological power do psychiatrists and psychologists ignore them? Let me explain.

Psychology and psychiatry are disciplines of science. They treat mental illness through the body, not the spirit. They do not recognise the spirit so have no understanding of the conditions they are trying to treat.

Science ignores the human spirit because it is not subject to the laws of physics, chemistry and biology. Anything outside those laws is outside science so is labelled, anti-science.

Psychiatry and psychology do not consider or accept anything that is anti-science. This is why they have little success with mental illness because it is in the spirit, which is anti-science, so ignored.

There is great irony in psychologists and psychiatrists ignoring the spirit, given the etymology of the words 'psychology' and 'psychiatry'. Let me show you.

'Psychology and Psychiatry' come from the Greek word *'Psyche'*. The definition of *'Psyche'* refers to the human *'mind and spirit.'*

'Psychotic' and *'Psychiatric'* consider the mental side of the human psyche.

'Psychic', considers the spiritual aspect of our 'Psyche'.

The original definition of the term, 'psyche' includes the mind and the spirit! Who knew? Until psychology and psychiatry embrace the full definition of the word 'psyche' which defines their own profession, they will not unravel the mysteries of mental illness, nor will they find a cure. They will remain forever between a rock and a hard place of their own making.

Imagine if medical science tested the ten commandments. It would lead to widespread recovery from mental illness. Psychologists and psychiatrists would be at the forefront of an outbreak of healing. The nation would be resilient against mental illness, it would become a rarity as it once was, a thing of the past. How amazing would that be?

Not for the pharmaceutical industry. They would be horrified because mental illness is a lucrative market. Recurrent, persistent and incurable diseases that require ongoing treatment with no expectation of recovery generate healthy profits from unhealthy people.

The pharmaceutical industry has no financial incentive to cure mental illness because there are no profits to be made out of healthy people. Where is the profit in that?

Medical science is dependent on the pharmaceutical industry as the pharmaceutical industry is dependent on medical science. Neither will bite the hand that feeds it. Treating chronic conditions for many years with pharmaceutical medications offering no expectation of a cure, as with mental health, is the fiscal sweet spot for the pharmaceutical industry and medical science. Why upset such a lucrative sweet spot?

That is why psychologists and psychiatrists will not test the spiritual power of the ten commandments, because they might just work, and that would upset everything!

Let us unlock each of the 10 commandments one at a time and see how incredible they are.

UNLOCKING
THE 1st COMMANDMENT

I BELIEVE YAHUAH ELOHIM IS CREATOR OF
HEAVEN AND EARTH. I SHALL HAVE NO OTHER
ELOHIM BEFORE HIM!

The Creator tells us in the first commandment His true name, which is *'Yahuah Elohim'*. So lost have the commandments been, very few souls even know the true name of their Creator. The Masorite Jews removed the Creator's name from the Creator's own book over a thousand years ago. This was not a slight oversight or mistake for they edited it out over six thousand eight hundred times. They meant to remove it, and they claim to be God's people? That is a circle that no one can square.

The true name was hidden by the Jews, so it is not surprising no one knows it. Look in any Bible or Torah and the name of the Creator 'Yahuah Elohim' is not there. It was for thousands of years but now it is gone. So why did they remove it?

The Pharisee Jews knew His true name has great spiritual power. They wanted that power for themselves. If that power was made available to everyone, as the Creator intended, what need or purpose would there be for the Pharisee religion, or any religion for that matter? The answer is none!

Humankind would be going directly to the Creator for their spiritual health without going near religion. That is exactly what I champion in this book.

The Creator's name has been replaced with 'Adonai' which is a Hebrew title meaning Lord. In the Bible it is replaced with titles such as Lord, God, God Almighty, the Almighty, or Lord God. We are not asked to call upon titles in which there is no power but His name, in which there is.

The Creator's name is Yahuah, and His title is 'Elohim,' which means spiritual beings.

Elohim is plural as it includes His Son, the Messiah even though He would not become flesh and dwell on earth for another 1,700 years, after writing the commandments on tablets of stone and giving them to Moses.

Believers in Yahuah Elohim are cared for and spiritually protected by Him. Angelic beings are appointed to watch over those who are His. They become Yahuah's spiritual family whilst living on earth in physical bodies, and members of His eternal family in the age to come.

Believers in Yahuah Elohim have the spirit of Yahuah Elohim, who is called the Ruach ha Kodesh, dwelling within them. Yahuah's own are called Yahudim, for our name is found in His.

The Yahudim are brothers and sisters of one spiritual family. We are a family that has nothing to do with religion. We are not separated by race, colour of skin, or nationality. Each of us is blood related directly to the Creator which means we are all blood related to each other. We share, care, teach and support each other. It is a quiet, gentle and sincere bond for we know we shall all know each other forever.

Entities in the spiritual realm from Archangels, to Cherubim, Seraphim, to demons, all know the Creator's name. We are to call upon His name, not His title because the power is in His name not His title. Who is to call upon His name?

"Come to me, all you who are weary and burdened, and I will give you rest. Take my yoke upon you and learn from me, For I am gentle and humble in heart, and you will find rest for your souls. For my yoke is easy and my burden is light."

The commandments are written for those who are weary and burdened, those struggling through life suffering from mental illness, chronic sickness, poverty, injustice and misfortune. He calls the forgotten and the lowly, whose lives are hard, for they are the ones who are under spiritual attack. They are the ones whose lives will be transformed by His commandments.

It is written, seek and you will find. Seek what, and what is there to find? Seek the Creator of our spirit through the ten commandments and you will find healing and rest for your soul.

Notice how the rich and famous were not called. They have wealth and fame to comfort them. They have no reason to turn to Yahuah Elohim for they have their false gods of money, power, fame, vanity and pride to heal their wounds.

It is written,

It is easier for a camel to pass through the eye of a needle than for a rich man to enter the gates of heaven.

Yahuah Elohim offers rest for the weary, healing to the sick and abundance to the poor. If life is wearisome and burdened then the commandments are for you. He knows you and all your needs. Through the commandments you can reach out spiritually and have all your needs met.

He wants to free you from your burdens so you can live the life He planned for you in the beginning, but you must seek Him, not the other way around. He will not help uninvited for that would violate your free will to choose or not choose Him. You must ask, which is to seek, then you will find and receive.

Keeping the commandments is seen in heaven by angelic beings for it is written,

There is more rejoicing in heaven in the presence of the angels of Yahuah Elohim over one sinner who repents than ninety-nine righteous people.

We are told to have no other Elohim or gods, but Him. What other gods are there? Money, fame, power, and pride are the big ones. These are the false gods of this world that many choose to worship in place of the Creator. False gods promise much yet seldom deliver.

False gods belong to Satan. Many worshippers of false gods often become obsessed with money, fame and power, and lose everything of true value in their devotion.

There is nothing wrong with money, fame and power! Many who keep the ten commandments have a great deal of money, fame and power given to them to fulfil their purpose. Many in the Dead Sea Scrolls were exceedingly rich and powerful.

When the Yahudim become rich and powerful, as many do, they are not at risk from false gods because it was not the false gods who gave them the wealth and power.

Our wealth and power comes from the commandments. We may be in the world but are not of the world. Our spiritual DNA is quite different. Spiritually we are separate from the world and protected from negative spiritual forces because our beliefs are supernaturally positive.

The most powerful beliefs we can have are those in Yahuah Elohim because they invite His spirit to dwell within ours. No belief gets more powerful than that.

UNLOCKING
THE 2nd COMMANDMENT

*I SHALL NOT MAKE FOR MYSELF ANY IMAGE IN THE FORM
OF ANYTHING IN HEAVEN ABOVE, OR ON EARTH
BENEATH, OR IN THE WATERS BELOW. I SHALL
NOT BOW DOWN TO THEM OR
WORSHIP THEM.*

This commandment separates spiritual health from religious practice. We are told not to make anything in any shape or form to represent our spiritual relationship with Yahuah Elohim, nor are we to bow down and worship them.

Religion is awash with icons, effigies and relics in all shapes and sizes. Churches are full of objects of devotion for the devout to bow down and worship.

This means religious worship is not toward the Creator, Yahuah Elohim for He tells us not to do these things. By their own scriptures their devotion is satanic. Breaking the commandments is sinful and sin harms the spirit. We are not to worship manmade objects because nothing humankind can make can ever be holy.

To worship before a cross, a depiction of the crucifixion or statue of the virgin Mary is to worship a worldly object. Worldly objects belong to the *'Prince of this World'*, who is Satan. Satan means adversary. Doing what the commandments tell us not to is to be adversarial, that is to be satanic.

Satan is not a demon. He is a spiritual entity whose original name was Gadre'el and was once a covering angel in the Garden of Eden that is within the earth. He was expelled from the garden because he sinned. This was the very first sin on earth and was the sin of pride.

Gadre'el, Satan, deceived Adam and Eve and now roams the earth in spiritual form, seeking to devour souls. How do we know this?

159

In the scroll of Peter it is written,

Be sober, be vigilant; because your adversary Satan the devil, as a roaring lion, walketh about, seeking whom he may devour:

Demons are under the dominion of Gadre'el, Satan and will devour any hapless soul that is without protection. Satan was given dominion over the demons so they may fulfil their purpose on earth. So, what is their purpose?

Their purpose is to provoke us into using our free will. The choice is between Yahuah Elohim and His angelic beings or Satan and his demons. That is the choice. There is not third option. This choice the ultimate purpose of free will and has eternal consequences.

Gadre'el, as in Satan, did not fall from heaven. He is not a fallen Watcher angel for if he was, he would be in the abyss of condemnation with all the other fallen Watcher angels. Satan did not procreate with human women as the fallen Watcher angels did'. Gadre'el, Satan, did not fall from heaven but was evicted from the Garden of Eden which is within the earth.

Satan still has access to the council of heaven and can still speak to the Creator, Yahuah Elohim, in the heavenly realm, even to this day. The Creator has made Satan Prince of this World and given to him all the worldly things with in it including demons. The world today belongs to Satan, and will until the end of the age, so he may fulfil his purpose.

When a devoutly religious person is fervently worshipping at the foot of a crucifix, or a statue of Mary and child, they are worshipping a worldly object. Worshipping worldly objects is to worship the prince of this world to whom all the worldly objects belong, and that is Satan. It is not complicated!

I seek not to offend the Christian community, though I seem to have a gift for it, but seek only to make known the truth according to their own scriptures. The truth is not hidden but writ large in the ten commandments I am showing you now.

Religion does not come from the Bible nor from the Dead Sea Scrolls. It is a practice that came from the fallen Watcher angels and their Nephilim hybrid human offspring. That is why there are so many different types of religion all worshiping different types of gods, all claiming to be the one true religion with the one true god.

The two hundred fallen angels set themselves up as gods over humankind, demanded tribute, obedience and sacrifice, even to the sacrificing of their children. This is the origin of religion.

Most Nephilim hybrid humans were destroyed in the flood in the days of Noah, but some survived as did their religious practices. Religious practice is therefore not holy for fallen angels lost their holy status. Humankind is not holy, nor can anything he makes become holy, nor the traditions he invents or the ceremonies he performs. There is no holiness in the practice of religion, only in a one-to-one relationship with the Creator.

The Church of England does not belong to Yahuah Elohim. It is worldly and belongs to Satan. It has land, property, worldly assets and presides over worldly laws through its bishops, who have seats in the government, specifically, the House of Lords.

It cannot preside over worldly laws and at the same time preside over spiritual laws. No one can serve two masters, no one can serve the Prince of this World and Yahuah Elohim and certainly not at the same time.

Yahuah Elohim does not work through religions because religions, by their nature are worldly, not spiritual. If Yahuah Elohim worked through religion, it would put Him on the same side as Satan so Satan would no longer be an adversary; Satan would be out of a job! The Creator works through the spirits of the Yahudim, those human souls who know Him, and they have nothing to do with religion.

A spiritual relationship with Yahuah is direct. It is one to one. It is a quiet and personal matter; it is spiritual. Religion would only get in the way.

I understand how many are attracted by the grandeur and sense of occasion that is synonymous with religious ceremonies. Remember, when substance is gone, all that's left is the ceremony. Ceremonies often become overly grandiose and splendid to compensate for the fact that there is no substance left.

Religious congregants face the dilemma whether to serve religious laws or Yahuah's laws. It is a stark choice with eternal consequences for this is your gift of free will in action. It is not possible to serve religion and Yahuah Elohim at the same time for no one can serve two masters. We all have free will to choose our life's path. Choose well dear friend.

UNLOCKING
THE 3rd COMMANDMENT

I SHALL NOT MISUSE THE NAME OF 'YAHUAH ELOHIM'.

Do not be misled by the brevity of this commandment. It has unexpected complexity and a great deal of hidden power.

We are not to misuse the name of the Creator. Few today even know the name of the Creator. Thankfully, you now do! How can a name no one knows be misused?

This commandment has been misunderstood for generations, because the name of the Creator was lost for over a thousand years. The Jews substituted the true name of 'Yahuah Elohim' for 'Adonai' which is a title, meaning lord. So, what is wrong with calling the Creator 'Adonai', or 'Lord'?

Lord, or Adonai in Hebrew is also translated as Ba'al. Ba'al is used as a title for Lord, or false gods worshipped in Biblical times that the Creator warns us against. Ba'al refers to the prince of demons, from where we get Ba'al zebub, the lord of the flies.

Removing the Creator's true name from His own book and replacing it with Ba'al zebub, lord of the flies, as in Adonai, is lawless and wrong. How must Yahuah feel toward the Rabbinic Jews having removed His name, and replaced it with the name of the false god, Ba'al? How strange the Jews left Satan's name untouched.

Elohim is the correct title for the Creator and happens to be plural. The Creator has a Son, the Messiah who became flesh and dwelt among us. The Son came in the name of the Father which means His name must be in the Father's. His name is Yahusha ha Mashiach, (Yahusha the Messiah), which clearly is in the name of Yahuah.

163

The name 'Jesus' is not in the name Yahuah. We cannot get Jesus Christ out of the name 'Yahuah Elohim' no matter how we rearrange the letters. With the name Yahusha, we clearly can. The scriptures tell us no other name is more powerful. Do you not then think it is important we at least get the name right?

Some believe this commandment is telling us not to misuse His name as a profanity like, God damn it, for God's sake, Jesus Christ, or for Christ's sake. I dislike profanity, but profanity is not what this commandment is about.

To misuse the name of Yahuah is to mislead people into breaking His commandments believing they are pleasing Him. Let me explain. A vicar calls the faithful to kneel or bow their heads in worship before a crucifix. This is not a righteous act but a lawless one. Doing this in the name of Yahuah Elohim is to misuse Yahuah's name. Such worship is to break His commandments. This is what we are warned not to do.

A Roman Catholic priest inviting someone to confess their sins believing the priest can forgive them of their sins is another misuse of Yahuah's name. We are told not to do these things because they are sinful and Satanic.

Mortal men cannot forgive each other's sins against Yahuah. Only Yahuah can forgive us our sins against Him. Promising forgiveness when it is not ours to give is a misuse of Yahuah's name. This is what we are warned not to do.

Sunday worship is another misuse of His name, for Sunday or Sun's-day is the day of pagan worship to the Sun-God. The commandments tell us to keep Shabbat as our day of rest, which is a Saturday. I have more to share with you on this shortly. Leading people to worship on Sunday is lawless and another misuse of His name.

What about Christmas? Christmas is surely not to misuse His name, is it? All the churches do it so surely it must be spiritually lawful and done rightly in His name? Not so!

164

Christmas is a pagan tradition and violates the commandments. It is not in the Bible, nor the Torah, nor the Dead Sea Scrolls, nor is it listed as one of Yahuah's holy days.

The term, Holy-days is where we get the word holiday. Christmas is not a holiday but a pagan festival celebrating the winter equinox. This is how easy it is to be misled by religion to break His commandments, especially if we don't know what those commandments are.

Surely the Messiah was born in December? I am afraid not! The Messiah was born on the feast of Shavuot which, on the Gregorian calendar changes a little each year but normally falls around late May or early June. How do we know Shavuot is when Yahusha ha Mashiach was born? The Dead Sea Scrolls and the New Testament scrolls tell us.

Christmas is pagan which begs the question as to what would happen to Christianity if the truth that is in the Dead Sea Scrolls were made public? The busiest time of the year for churches would be rendered meaningless.

Shepherds do not spend nights in their fields in December but in the lambing season during April and May. The Messiah is the Lamb of God, yet Christianity seems to have no idea when lambs are born. Lambs are not born in December, but in the lambing season.

Yahusha ha Mashiach was born in Bethlehem during the lambing season, on the feast of Shavuot. Bethlehem is where the lambs were bred for sacrifice in the temple in Jerusalem, the very place the Messiah was sacrificed as the Lamb of God for humankind. The parallels are not meant to go unnoticed.

How would you feel if your family decided to celebrate your birthday on someone else's birthday? The 25th of December is a pagan day of worship for the Saturnalia, the Sun God and his winter equinox. Imagine how the Creator feels toward Christians celebrating His birthday on the birthday of the false Sun God.

Infant baptisms are another misuse of His name. It makes no spiritual sense to baptise infants for they are sanctified by their innocence. They do not need to be baptised. Telling parents to Christen their babies because it pleases the Creator is to misuse the name of Yahuah. He tells us He does not want this, so don't do it.

Easter is another misuse of Yahuah's name. The word Easter is from the Nephilim goddess 'Ishtar', the goddess of fertility, hence her eggs and rabbits. The participation of male and female prostitutes was common practice during Ishtar worship. Not something I have seen in a Church of England Easter service, well not yet anyway.

The more the truth is revealed the plainer it is to see that religion has nothing to do with the commandments. I seek not to offend the Christians or the Jews because my battle is not with flesh and blood but against principalities, against powers, against the rulers of the darkness of this world.

My battle is against spiritual wickedness in high places. So, if I have offended you, please don't take it personally, I was aiming much higher.

Many believe the name we are not to misuse is the name, Jesus Christ. Allow me to challenge your belief on this as gently as I can. Like I say, I mean not to offend.

Let us start by agreeing that Jesus Christ was a real person who lived two thousand years ago in Israel. Let us also agree that He was the Son of Yahuah Elohim, the long-awaited Messiah who was made flesh and dwelt among us. We can at least start off on the same page.

First question; how is it possible for His name to be Jesus when the letter 'J' did not come into existence until the 1500s? The Messiah, we have already agreed, lived two thousand years ago. So, if the letters in His name were not invented for another 1,500 years, how can His name be Jesus? The name Jesus becomes problematic when applying it to the Messiah.

Being made flesh and dwelling among us 1,500 years before the letter 'J' came into existence means the Messiah must have already had a name which we are told is the most powerful name in heaven and on earth. Do you see the problem?

Messiah existed before creation for creation was made through Him. The name 'Jesus', is not found in the name of the Creator, or even on earth before the 1500s. The name 'Jesus' is another manmade invention. The Messiah said.

"I come in the name of the Father
for I am in the Father as He is in Me."

Not with the name Jesus he isn't! The name 'Jesus' is not in the name of Yahuah Elohim. The name Yahusha is.

Let me unlock the mystery of the Creator's name for you. The root of the Creator's name, Yahuah, is 'Yah', meaning I am.

'Yah' is found in the name, *Yah*-uah, and in *Yah*-usha, and in *Yah*-udim.

Those who belong to the Creator are Yahudim. The name 'Yahudim' did not fall off the shelf for all names are specific and have power and meaning. Let us unpack the name, Yahudim.

The Creator's name is Yahuah. The word *'YAH-HU'* means salvation, *'YAH-HUD'* is one who is saved and the plural of *'YAHUD'* is *'YAHUDIM'*. There we have it. We are the ones who are saved spiritually through Him! That is what the name 'Yahudim' means. To be Yahudim is to have the ultimate spiritual health.

Let us expand this to prove names have meaning. According to the Dead Sea Scrolls, Adam was the first man on earth. The name 'Adam' means 'Man'. What if the Creator had been momentarily distracted and named him Frank? What difference would that have made?

The name Frank in Latin is Francis, meaning Frenchman. Unless Adam was born in France, which I can assure you he wasn't, the meaning of his name would be nonsensical for it would conflict with its meaning.

It would not work; it would be out of context and would undermine the belief that creation was meticulously planned and perfectly constructed. Names matter! Names have meanings. Your name is not random either, for it also has a meaning.

Consider names with the letters, 'EL' in them, such as Elizabeth and Joel. Who today knows the meaning or relevance of the letters 'EL' in a name? Very few I imagine. The letters 'EL' come from the Hebrew word, 'Elohim' the very title of the Creator. Who knew? Their name reveals an aspect of Yahuah Elohim.

How many souls with 'EL' in their name realise their name is directly associated with Yahuah Elohim, the true name of the Creator? This must be one of the best-kept secrets ever. Let me share with you their original Hebrew meanings.

- Joel means, Yahuah is Elohim.
- Adelle means, Elohim is Eternal
- Noel means, Elohim's birthday hence Noel at Christmas.
- Elizabeth means, Elohim is my oath,
- Michael means, he who is like Elohim
- Daniel means, Elohim is my judge
- Rachel means, ewe or little lamb of Elohim
- Ella means, goddess or female beauty of Elohim

The names of angels, fallen angels and archangels also have 'EL' in them, as revealed by the Dead Sea Scrolls. This is no accident nor is it random. Everything has its place in creation, even names. The names and meanings of the seven Archangels known also as the Angels of the Presence, in the heavenly realm overseeing creation are as follows.

- Michael means, he who is like Elohim
- Raphael means, Elohim has healed
- Gabriel means, Elohim is my strength
- Uriel means, Elohim is my light
- Saraqael means, noble of Elohim
- Raguel means, a friend of Elohim
- Remiel means, the thunder of Elohim.

Fallen Watcher angels also had 'EL' in them, for they were once holy in the heavenly realm. Before they fell, they were servants of Yahuah Elohim. Let me share the names of their leaders with you so you can know these things for yourself.

The names of some of the fallen Watcher angels were,

- Azazel
- Arakiel
- Baraqiel
- Rame'el
- Kokabi'el
- Tamiel
- Exeke'el
- Sariel

Their names all express some aspect of Yahuah Elohim, which is why they have 'EL' in them. These Watcher angels fell from their heavenly estate to earth in the days of Jared, originally Yar'ed, and procreated with human women.

Every fallen angel is currently incarcerated in the Abyss of Condemnation deep within the earth awaiting judgement. Names matter! Your name matters so cherish it and make it a name to be proud of.

Christian denominations come in their own name. Yahuah's name is not found in the names of the Roman Catholics, Protestants, Methodists, Baptists, Presbyterians, Pentecostals, Lutherans, Quakers, Church of England or Evangelicals, for as lovely as they all may be, they come in their own name, for Yahuah's name is not in them.

Nothing is named by chance or by accident. Humankind must learn to stop going around just making stuff up. Let us look at a few more names to know what I say is true.

Abram was a Patriarch in the Dead Sea Scrolls and the Bible. The Creator changed Abram's name by putting His name in Abram's, creating Abr-*Yah*-ham. This became *'Abraham'*. Abraham's wife Sarai's name was changed to Sar*Yah*, becoming *'Sarah'*.

The Creator called Himself *'Yah'* when He appeared to Moses at the burning bush. This is when He told Moses to lead the Hebrews out of Egypt. Moses asked, who are you that I may tell the Hebrews who sent me? The Creator said,

"Hy-Yah Ashar Hy-Yah",
'I am who I am'.

The Creator called Himself *'Yah'*, which means, *'I am!'* No other name would meaningfully describe who and what He is. What if the Creator said His name was Tom? That would be a problem because Tom or Thomas means twin. Can you see the problem?

The name Benjamin is 'Ben-*Yah*-Min'. 'Ben' means son, 'Yah' is the name of the Creator and 'Min' is plural. Benjamin means *'sons of Yah.'* Like I say, names have meanings which I find endlessly fascinating.

The prophet Isaiah's real name in Hebrew is *'Yesha-yah-u'*. When his name is translated from Hebrew into Greek it becomes Isaiah, and the Creator's name is lost in the translation. Isaiah's name loses its etymological meaning and spiritual significance. Therefore, we can't go around naming things willy-nilly.

Cartographers in the 18th and 19th century, whilst mapping out the earth, changed many original place names, charting the new world as they saw it. They edified themselves and their patrons by renaming places.

Place names lost their original meaning and knowledge of historical events was lost. Mount Hermon is an example of a place name recording an extra-terrestrial encounter between angelic beings and this realm that remains unchanged.

The name Hermon is the name of the Mount where the fallen angels came to earth. The name Hermon means to consecrate or to forfeit, as in an oath. The fallen Watcher angels made an oath between themselves to jointly take the blame for what they were about to do in violating the laws of procreation, on Mount Hermon.

The name of Mount Hermon has remained unchanged and the connection between this world and the falling of the angels from the heavenly realm has been preserved in its etymology.

You may ask why I refer often back to the Hebrew language. Firstly, the Dead Sea Scrolls were written in Hebrew, and I want to retain the text's original meanings wherever I can.

Secondly, Hebrew is the language of the heavenly realm and the language of creation. Hebrew is the language of angels and demons. It is the language of the Nephilim; it is the language of the spiritual realm.

Thirdly, it was the original language on earth until the event at the tower of Babel. It is from the tower of 'Babel', we get the word babble, when languages became divided. Even the word 'babble' has a fascinating etymology.

Languages share a common origin which we see by their similarities. The number 'nine' in English, is Neuf in French, in German it is Neun, in Italian it is Nove and in Spanish it is Nueve. If languages do not have a common origin, why are so many words similar as we see with the number nine?

You may ask, if all languages are connected and come from the same Hebrew origin, where is the connection between English and Hebrew? Let me show you.

The first two letters in the Hebrew alphabet are, Aleph and Bet. Put them together and we get 'alphabet', the foundation of the English language. There is the connection between English and the Hebrew language.

Tech giants in Silicon Valley know the power of Yahuah's name. Search engine *Yah-Hoo* did not call itself that by accident. They know Yahuah Elohim is omniscient, as in all-knowing, omnipresent as in everywhere all the time, and omnipotent as in all-powerful, and is the very image Yahoo seeks to portray for itself.

Whatever your name, treasure it, make it yours, make it great, make it honourable, be proud of it, be known by your name. Be proud to be you for you are made in the Creator's image.

Our ultimate destiny is to have our name written in the book of life, eternal life, which is kept in the heavenly realm. When your name is written there, you have made it!

UNLOCKING
THE 4th COMMANDMENT

*I SHALL REMEMBER THE SABBATH DAY. I SHALL KEEP IT
HOLY. SIX DAYS SHALL I LABOUR AND DO ALL
MY WORK, BUT THE SEVENTH DAY IS A
SABBATH, TO YAHUAH ELOHIM.
ON IT I SHALL DO NO WORK.*

Keeping the Sabbath, or in Hebrew, Shabbat is to set aside one day every week to rest from our labour. That day is Saturday, not Sunday. How difficult is that?

Shabbat is Hebrew for the seventh day, which is the last day of the week, it is a time for rest. Keeping Shabbat has immense spiritual significance because it commemorates the completion of the creation week.

Keeping Shabbat for the Yahudim is a quiet and private matter. Honouring this day is between you and the Creator. That's it! Yahuah Elohim sees you keeping Shabbat as do the angels because Shabbat is kept in the heavenly realm, at the same time as we keep it here on earth.

The Messiah tells us,

*The sabbath was made for man, and not man for the sabbath:
Therefore, the Messiah is Elohim also of the sabbath.*

The Messiah is not Elohim of Sunday. Keeping shabbat is key to spiritual health. It is a day of relaxation, study, quiet contemplation, and reflection. It is a day to collect our thoughts, take a breath and replenish our body and spirit. Shabbat generates positive spiritual energy needed for healing, staying well and staying protected.

Shabbat is a time for family, friends, good food and good wine, it is a moment to celebrate, having made it successfully through another week. It is a day for righting wrongs, apologising, and forgiving where

173

necessary. It is a time for giving thanks for what we have, asking for answers to problems we may be facing and guidance through difficult times.

It is a time to make our wants known to Yahuah Elohim so He can help us. He keeps Shabbat too, so not only will He hear you He may well ask you to do things for Him. He may lay on your heart obligations and acts of kindness, generosity, and support He wants you to do for others who may be struggling. Shabbat is a time to check our spiritual compass. How difficult or unpleasant is that?

If Shabbat is a day of rest, what are we able to do on it? Certain Jewish groups have turned Shabbat into a day of oppressive denial and slavish obedience, saying that we are not to cook, wash up, listen to the radio, turn on the light, travel, answer the phone, buy something, paint, play the piano, play sport, sail, ride a horse, swim and on it goes. They turn Shabbat into a day of inert boredom, spending it doing absolutely nothing.

The commandments say that we are to labour for six days and rest from our labours on Shabbat. Leisure pursuits are not labours. Taking the children or grandchildren out for a lovely time and buying them ice-cream or little treats is part of Shabbat. It is to be enjoyed for it is a rest from six days of labour. We are not to work for money, which is what we have done for the previous six days.

Shabbat celebrates the first complete week of creation from where the seven-day week comes. If creation did not happen in seven days, then where did the seven-day week come from? How come, thousands of years later, we still keep it? There has never been a time in history without it.

Shabbat has been observed continuously in the heavenly realm and on earth from the beginning of time. Adam and Eve kept Shabbat in the garden of Eden, and it is kept by the Yahudim still. It is prophesied to be kept continually on earth until the end of this age. It is not possible to keep the commandments without keeping Shabbat.

Shabbat gives us an entire day to focus on positive thoughts and beliefs and our relationship with the Creator. Demons cannot tolerate Shabbat or those who keep it, for they cannot tolerate positive energy generated on a day that is appointed by law to be positive in energy. Shabbat is a protection over us and a weapon of spiritual warfare against dark forces seeking to harm us.

Demons will try and prevent a soul from keeping Shabbat because it is spiritually lawful. Those who keep the spiritual laws have power and authority over demons. That is why demons try and prevent souls from keeping any of the laws.

Shabbat separates the Yahudim from religion. The Jews do keep Shabbat but do not believe in Yahusha ha Mashiach, the Messiah, so cannot get past the first commandment. If you can't get past the first commandment, the other nine are of little consequence or salvation.

The Church of England and the Roman Catholic Church just don't keep Shabbat, period!

Those unable to keep Shabbat because of work commitments can talk to the Creator somewhere quiet and private. He hears you, knows you and knows your situation.

He already knows everything about you including what you are going to ask. He is waiting for you already. Make your request known. Ask Him to make Shabbat possible and then just wait and watch.

In time, when it is right, you will see your circumstances change and the opportunity to keep Shabbat will come. I have seen this happen often.

UNLOCKING
THE 5th COMMANDMENT

I WILL HONOUR MY FATHER AND MOTHER, SO
THAT I MAY LIVE LONG IN THE LAND
YAHUAH ELOHIM HAS GIVEN ME.

Fig. 11

MOTHERHOOD
Painting by Rosa-Lee Tuffney

Children are to honour their parents. The strongest spiritual connection on earth is between parents and their children. When family relationships break down, it injures the spirits of the parents and the children.

Mental health conditions often improve when broken family relationships are healed. The power of reconciliation is healing to the spirit because reconciliation is positive energy.

Parents instinctively care for their young. The young do not always instinctively care for their parents, especially when they are old. The purpose of this commandment is to remind the children of their spiritual obligation to care for their parents in old age, and to honour them.

Abandoning parents to others or to the state for their care is not honouring them. Many children in adulthood do not feel obligated to repay their spiritual debt to parents because they know nothing of the commandments that speak of this spiritual obligation.

Dishonouring parents brings negative spiritual energy into a person's life, adversely effecting their fortunes. When this happens, most will have no idea why. When this commandment is kept, the health of the spirit is restored, and quality of life is restored.

Few commandments bring a curse. This one does. Those who dishonour their parents will not live long and happy lives in old age. Misfortune, misery and poor health will befall them.

Honouring parents is not always easy, for some parents are not as loving and caring as we would have hoped. Most parents do their best. That does not mean they did right or did well. We need to forgive them if they fell short of our expectations. Having disappointing or difficult parents does not exonerate us from this commandment to honour them.

The more challenging the commandment, the greater the positive the energy, so the bigger the blessings. It takes no effort to be nice to someone who is nice in return. It is more challenging being nice to someone who is not nice in return. Honouring parents does not mean we have to like them or even agree with them. We are to honour them and show them respect, patience, and kindness. We are to see to their well-being and welfare. If you happen to like them, then that is a bonus.

Demons will exploit broken family relationships. They feed off broken relationships, agitate them and make them worse. Those who are wise will not allow demons to exploit such a vulnerability.

Remember, the more difficult the commandment the closer your relationship with Yahuah Elohim will be, and the greater the spiritual power you will have. Nothing goes unnoticed or unaccounted for. All your efforts are seen and measured. Everything we do and say matters, so it is always worth making that extra effort.

UNLOCKING
THE 6th COMMANDMENT

I SHALL NOT COMMIT MURDER

No one gets away with murder. The dark spiritual energy generated by murder does not disappear or lessen over time. Witnessed or not, dark energy from murder cannot be hidden from Yahuah Elohim.

The first law of thermodynamics states that energy cannot be created out of nothing, nor can it be destroyed. It can only be transferred from one form to another. The act of murder releases a burst of dark spiritual energy. Dark energy clings to the soul of a murderer bringing rot and decay.

Taking a life is murder. Abortion is to take a life. There are exceptions to abortion if the mother's life is at risk, or when conception is a Satanic act and not of the Creator. Violent rape, or when a minor is raped or there has been incest are Satanic conceptions. In these instances, talking to the Creator and listening through intuition, dreams, and revelation will guide us to do the lawful thing. What we are to do will be laid on our heart. Some situations do not have easy answers. That is why we turn to Him.

Abortion for non-medical, non-exceptional reasons such as convenience, or exposure to unfaithfulness, generates dark energy for it is the taking of a life that would otherwise be viable.

I am not here to judge any mother for any reason for having an abortion. I am no judge over anyone because I have made more mistakes than most. But there is one who will judge you and me. The life that was taken through abortion belongs to Him, not you nor me!

I, nor anyone else can judge another for none of us know the mind of the Creator. What I can do is explain what happens spiritually when a life is taken. There are spiritual consequences few of us know, that we should all know about because they affect our spiritual health and destiny.

Life is not ours to take, ever! Taking a life that does not belong to us but is precious to Yahuah Elohim releases a huge amount of dark energy that rots the soul from within. Over time, many who have committed murder or had an abortion, find themselves deeply troubled in their mind and in their dreams. This deep-seated anxiety is the rotting of the soul.

They become increasingly reflective on the life that was taken, remorseful and troubled in their spirit. Dark energy from taking a life does not disappear nor can it be destroyed, nor can it be hidden or made benign.

It is a debt that will be accounted for on our day of judgement. It is a debt that will be settled one way or another. An eye for an eye and a tooth for a tooth, so it is with a life for a life.

There is a way out! Dark energy from taking a life can be atoned for. The debt can be settled in this life without losing our life. It is through a spiritual process of confession, repentance, and forgiveness.

To repent, we need to confess to Yahuah Elohim. Repentance is one to one, it is personal and private. Yahuah was there at the time and saw everything that happened. We need to ask Him to forgive us for taking a life that was not ours to take but belonged to Him for all life is His. This is the only way of separating our soul from the dark energy we created by taking a life.

If we are contrite, and it is His will, and by His grace, He can forgive us. He can lift the debt of dark energy off us and take it away. Only Yahuah Elohim can forgive murder for all life is His which means our debt is to Him. He is the giver and the taker of life.

All life is a gift from Yahuah Elohim. Even our own life is a gift from Him, and we do not have the right to even take our own life. It is not ours to take because He gave it to us as a gift.

He delighted in making each one of us in His image. He hates it when someone destroys what belongs to Him and what He took pleasure in creating for Himself.

Life on earth is messy and accidents happen. If a life has been taken through a poor decision, lack of judgement, a moment of madness, or an accident, then we can atone for what we have done, we can ask to be forgiven. No one is beyond His forgiveness if our heart is repentant.

Yahuah Elohim hears the prayers and the confessions of those who belong to Him and ignores those who do not. Yahuah knows those who know Him. Those who belong to Him know He is there and how to speak to Him. They know they can talk to Him and that they will be heard. They know also that it is possible to be forgiven, even if a life has been taken.

To know Him is to learn of Him. He tells us,

"Come to me, all you who are weary and burdened, and I will give you rest. Take my yoke upon you and learn from me,
For I am gentle and humble in heart, and you will
find rest for your souls. For my yoke is easy
and my burden is light."

We need to learn of Him if we are to know of Him and believe in Him. There is a reading list at the back of this book that will give you all the material you could ever want to learn of Yahuah Elohim. There is a lifetime of spiritual nourishment to be enjoyed.

Speaking to Yahuah Elohim from the heart, being truly repentant and asking to be forgiven, is the only way the debt of taking someone's life can be paid for. We offer our life to Him as payment.

We offer our life to be in His service. We offer ourselves, and if the offer is accepted, the debt can be repaid, over time, day by day, year by year for the rest of our lives. This way the debt can be paid off. It will not be there on the scales of justice come the day of judgment, and we still get to keep our lives for eternity.

Forgiveness depends on repentance. Repentance is to be truly sorry? Once forgiven, there is no condemnation. The debt is paid, it is gone. If we have offered our lives to Him in payment, and received forgiveness for murder, then come to our day of judgement, that debt will not be there.

The Dead Sea Scrolls tell of people who committed murder, sought forgiveness, and went on to live amazing lives. Moses, the greatest of all prophets, took a life and lived into old age doing extraordinary things.

King David killed combatants on the battlefield, starting with Goliath when he was just a teenager. When he was King he also had Uriah murdered by proxy on the battlefield by having Uriah take the front line.

David did this so he could take Uriah's bereaved wife Bathsheba, for himself. Their first child died to atone for taking Uriah's life. David then repented, and had a son with Bathsheba, called Solomon, who became the richest and wisest of all kings. There is a way back from taking a life by atoning for what we have done.

David went on to become a great king. A woman called 'Ya-el' killed Sisera, a military leader. Her life continued to be blessed.

If you have taken a life do not neglect or try to hide what you have done from Yahuah Elohim. Hiding it is impossible for He is omnipresent. He sees everything.

Hiding from Him what He saw, for He was there, is futile and will bring decay to the soul. Talk to Yahuah in the full assurance that He hears you. He saw what happened and is waiting for you to come to Him for forgiveness.

He will guide you toward repentance so you can be forgiven for what you have done. With a contrite and repentant heart, faith in Him, and with an offer of your own life, He will hear you and by His grace, forgive you so you may keep your life and be judged well come the day of judgement.

Either way, you will pay. It is better to settle now when you can, than try and sort it out on the day of judgement when there will be nothing more you can do.

Speak directly to Yahuah Elohim as if speaking to your father. He will hear and will speak back to you. He will speak through your thoughts and beliefs and will put ideas into your head. He will speak through your intuition and your dreams. He can put wisdom and understanding into your mind. He is very real and alive for those who know Him and turn to Him in troubled times.

Forgiveness removes sin as if it never existed. There is no spiritual record of it on earth or in heaven. There is no negative energy, no guilt or shame. If Yahuah can forgive you then you can forgive yourself.

Forgiveness leaves nothing for demons to exploit or feed off. If the sin has gone then so should the guilt and the shame. Do not allow demons to accuse you of guilt and shame for something that no longer exists. Do not be deceived by them.

Do not let fear, guilt and shame take root. Let them go. They are not fruits of the spirit but the currency of demons. Part of being forgiven is believing that you truly have been forgiven. Demons cannot bind you if they have nothing to bind you with. When the debt has been paid, it is gone, so let it go and move on.

Those who are wise in the spirit will settle their debts as soon as possible. They know when this life is over, we can RIP, rest in peace, without fear, looking forward to our day of judgement in the assurance we are Yahudim, we are saved.

Having wisdom in this life means we can be confident of what lies beyond, and by His grace, we will see eternal life. This is the outcome of spiritual health.

This book will help you with repentance and forgiveness. I can help you to restore your life and restore your spiritual health even if you have taken a life. With Yahuah Elohim, your best days are still ahead.

UNLOCKING
THE 7th COMMANDMENT

I SHALL NOT COMMIT ADULTERY

Adultery is lawless because it breaks the vows of marriage. Traditional marriage vows are a covenant between husband, wife and Yahuah Elohim. People ask, where is Yahuah Elohim in the traditional marriage vows? Yahuah Elohim invented marriage, and the vows! The concept of marriage comes from Him. In the Dead Sea Scrolls it is written.

"In the beginning, He made them male and female.
For this cause shall a man leave his father and mother
and shall cleave to his wife and they twain shall be one flesh.

What therefore Yahuah Elohim has joined
together, let not man put asunder. "

Traditional marriage vows end with, 'according to God's Holy Ordinance' which means 'according to 'Yahuah Elohim's commandments,' the ones we are unlocking right now.

Honouring marriage is part of the ten commandments. The seventh commandment forbids adultery because it is the other half of the marriage vows. The laws of Yahuah Elohim fit together perfectly.

Adultery is carnal. Love is spiritual. Adultery is never rooted in love. Adultery is always rooted in lust because love would not tempt a soul to break the ten commandments, lust, being carnal, will.

Adultery has a spiritual dimension. Negative spiritual energy is left by each partner upon the other. Demonic forces exploit negative energy and bring misfortune upon adulterers. Adulterers are often tempted into ever greater betrayal, ending in ever greater disaster.

Adultery gives demons the lawful right to harass, deceive and torment. The rich and famous and even princes have been brought low by the seductions of adulterous spirits leading them into betrayal, disaster, guilt and shame.

Marriages can be destroyed by adulterous spirits if given the opportunity. Marriages that survive seldom recover fully because trust is never the same after it has been broken. Trust is a fruit of the spirit. Adultery harms the spirit and spoils its fruit. Spiritual health cannot be achieved whilst in an adulterous relationship.

Some claim to have been driven to adultery by a loveless marriage.' If a marriage is over and there is no love, it can be ended without adultery. One is never an excuse for the other.

UNLOCKING
THE 8th COMMANDMENT

I SHALL NOT STEAL

Stealing is a crime; it is lawless on earth and in the heavenly realm. Stealing generates lawless energy rooted in guilt, shame, stress, anxiety, and fear of exposure which rots the spirit of the thief over time.

Shame, guilt, stress and anxiety can lead to mental illness, paranoia, substance abuse, addiction to gambling or pornography, emotional instability, low self-esteem, escapism, and unhealthy short-term relationships. These are all symptoms of a spirit in poor health that can be brought about by stealing.

Do not be tempted to steal. It is never worth it. There is always a way to get what we want lawfully. If you desire something you cannot afford, turn to Yahuah Elohim, and ask Him for it. If He agrees you need it, He will sort it for you. It does not get easier than that.

If He decides you do not need it, then forget it and move on. There is no point longing for something you do not need and cannot afford. Needing something is different from lusting after something. Lust and desire belong to the carnal-self and needs to be kept in check by a dominant spiritual-self.

Be content. Be thankful for what you have. These are fruits of the spirit. Do not be scared to ask Yahuah Elohim for the things you do want. The worst that will happen is that He will say no. He will be pleased you asked in the first place.

UNLOCKING
THE 9th COMMANDMENT

I SHALL NOT GIVE FALSE TESTIMONY
AGAINST MY NEIGHBOUR

A false testimony is a lie. Gossips are skilled at lying which is why they are best avoided. Gossips are also renowned for betraying confidence, which is another reason to avoid them.

Avoid those who talk too much, for when many words are used, deceit is not far behind. Conflict seldom starts by saying nothing but often by saying too much. Few are found guilty for what they have not said.

Beware of the temptation to speak too quickly, or too rashly, especially on social media platforms such as Twitter, Instagram, and Facebook. They are a gossip's charter. Tread carefully, speak thoughtfully. Think first, think again, then speak. We have two ears and one mouth. If we listen twice as much as we talk, then we will avoid a lot of trouble.

Anyone causing the innocent to suffer by giving a false witness will be held accountable for that suffering. Whatever suffering was brought upon the innocent by a loose tongue, or a malicious heart will find its way back to the
perpetrator.

If you have suffered because a false testimony was given against you, do not seek revenge. Revenge is a trap demons exploit. Yahuah Elohim saw it all. It is written in the ancient scrolls:

"Vengeance is mine, says Yahuah Elohim."

Ask Yahuah Elohim to settle your account. The innocent will be avenged. Debts will be paid. This is an eternal law. We do not have to get our own back because Yahuah Elohim will take righteous revenge on our behalf.

His righteous vengeance is always far more punitive and painful than anything we could deliver.

Let all thoughts of spite or vengeance go and leave the vengeance to Him. The guilty will not get away with it, ever!

Be ever mindful of what you say. The spoken word has unseen power. Our greatest vulnerability is a loose and reckless tongue. It can land us into trouble quicker than anything.

If we cannot say anything constructive, encouraging, or good, then say nothing at all. Remember, when many words are used, deceit is not far behind.

We have only to look at how many words are used in the terms and conditions of banks, credit card companies, social media platforms, insurance companies and contracts of employment to know that the devil hides in the details. The more details there are, the more he can hide.

UNLOCKING
THE 10th COMMANDMENT

I SHALL NOT COVET MY NEIGHBOUR'S HOUSE.
I SHALL NOT COVET MY NEIGHBOUR'S WIFE,
OR HIS MALE OR FEMALE SERVANT, HIS
OX OR DONKEY, OR ANYTHING THAT
BELONGS TO MY NEIGHBOUR.

To covet is to envy or to be jealous. Jealousy is toxic. It is often called the green-eyed monster, and for good reason. Jealousy is voracious and never satisfied. The more it is fed, the hungrier it is. Nothing good comes from being jealous of others, or of what they have.

The grass only 'appears' greener on the other side. The opposite of jealousy is contentment and gratefulness which are fruits of the spirit. Neglected spirits bear little fruit so can easily become jealous. A healthy spirit will bear a lot of fruit so is resilient against jealous thoughts.

Those who are wise in the spirit know they can have whatever they want in life, so jealousy has no hold over them. They have only to ask the Creator, Yahuah Elohim. In this way everything that is needed is within reach for those who are wise in the spirit.

Why be jealous of what someone else has when we know we have the power to reach out to Yahuah Elohim and have whatever we need whenever we need it.

The Creator tells us in Mark, 11.24,

Therefore, I tell you, whatever you ask for in prayer,
believe that you have received it, and it will be yours.

We have spiritual power which means nothing is beyond our reach. It is far more likely others will be jealous of us. If they want what we have, show them how and where they can have it for themselves. Share what you know.

We have the power to heal and cast out demons of mental illness. We have the keys to a life of joy, peace, and abundance. We know where to find the path to eternal life. Nothing we need is withheld from us. We can have whatever we want for it is written,

"Anyone healing in My name has My power, My authority and My permission to cast out demons and to heal. Anyone who is not against Me is for me." "If you love me, keep my commandments."

THE ORIGIN
OF THE 10 COMMANDMENTS

The origin of the ten commandments is supernatural and extra-terrestrial. They were written on tablets of stone by the finger of the Creator, Yahuah Elohim and given to Moses on Mount Sinai around 3,700 years ago.

The commandments are a gift for humankind, a covenant that leads to eternal life. They are the measure by which we will all be judged, giving us a lifetime to prepare, so we may be judged well. Those who are judged well will receive eternal life. Eternal life is the meaning of life on earth. The keys to eternal life are in the commandments which is why they are for all of us.

The commandments existed long before Yahuah Elohim gave them to Moses on the tablets of stone. They are spiritual laws that date back to the very beginning of time. They were kept by Adam and Eve in the Garden of Eden.

They were known to Enoch and to his great-grandson Noah, who built the Ark in the days of the flood. I am sharing with you the same commandments they had, they knew and kept.

The prophet Moses lived around 3,700 years ago. He was shown the secrets of creation and told to write down what he saw for the benefit of humankind so we could all know these things.

Moses was a Hebrew, born in Egypt when the Pharaoh had enslaved the Hebrews for fear of their increasing numbers, so decreed that all Hebrew male babies were to be killed at birth.

Yocheved, the mother of Moses, was desperate to save her baby son. She defied Pharoah's decree and after nursing him for a few months, laid Moses in a basket and left him to float among the reeds on the banks of the river Nile.

He was found and taken in by the daughter of Pharaoh who had gone to the waters of the Nile to bathe. This is where the term 'Moses Basket' comes from.

Fig. 12

MOSES BASKET

Moses grew up in Pharoah's palace and was well educated. Around the age of forty, he saw an Egyptian overseer beating a Hebrew slave and went to the slave's defence. In the struggle, Moses killed the Egyptian overseer.

The event was witnessed, so fearing prosecution, fled into the wilderness of Midian, modern Saudi Arabia. There he lived for forty years, marrying Zipporah, and having two sons, Gershom, and Eliezer. He made his living rearing sheep.

Around 80 years old, Moses witnessed the bizarre sight of a burning bush in the wilderness. Though on fire, the bush was not consumed by the fire. As he approached, he heard a voice calling him to return to Egypt. He was told to lead the Hebrews out of Egypt and out of slavery.

Moses, with help from his older brother Aaron, returned to Egypt. After many plagues against Pharoah, culminating in the Angel of Death killing the first born of all living creatures across Egypt, except for the Hebrews,

Moses and Aaron led the Hebrew nation out. They crossed the Red Sea where the waters famously parted and then into the wilderness of Midian, where he had been living for the previous forty years.

The Hebrew nation wandered in the wilderness for forty years. They settled for a time at the foot of Mount Sinai in the wilderness of Saudi Arabia.

Fig. 13

MOUNT SINAI

Mount Sinai is where Yahuah Elohim descended from the heavenly realm in a great cloud of fire, thunder and lightning and remained for many days. Eyewitnesses recorded the event as a terrifying extra-terrestrial encounter. The rock face on top of the mountain is still seen to be scorched to this day. Visit: Ron Wyatt archaeological research, for photographic evidence.

Moses was called up the mountain into the great cloud of fire, thunder, and lightning for forty days and nights with the Creator and angelic beings. This is when Moses wrote many of the Dead Sea Scrolls including the scroll of Jubilees. This is the scroll that reveals the spiritual forces behind mental illness.

Fig. 14

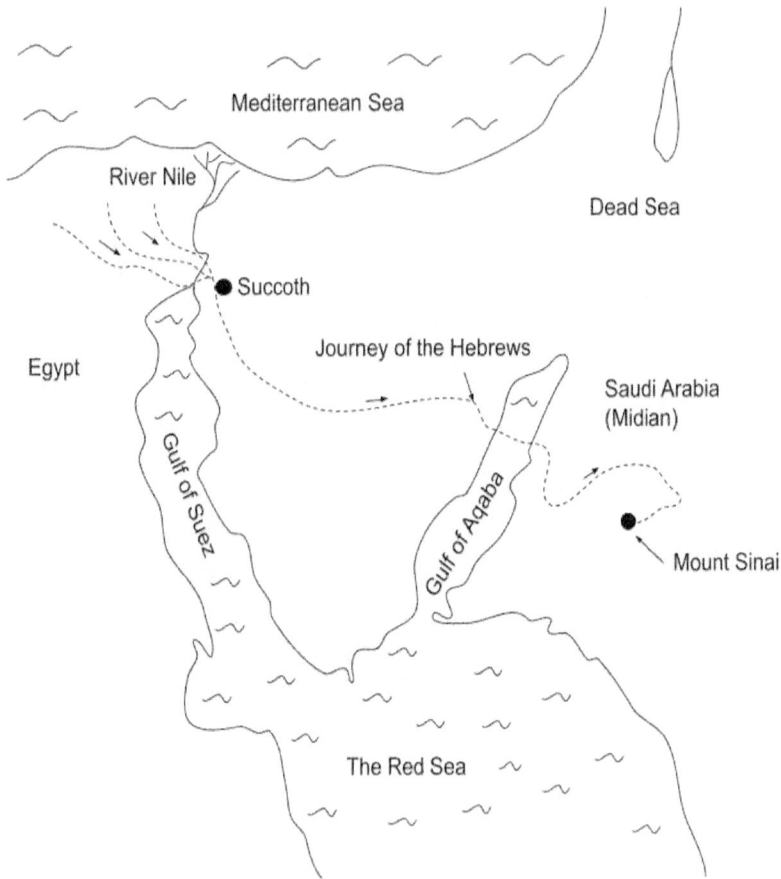

MAP TO MOUNT SINAI

An Angel of the Presence dictated to Moses, word for word what he was to write on the scrolls. How do we know this? We know because the original Hebrew scrolls have hundreds of secret messages and hidden codes buried in the original text that reveal the history of humankind in advance.

Every letter had to be perfectly placed for this to be possible. Moses could not have done this for he would have had to have known history in advance and been an expert in codes.

Hidden in the text are names, places and events that had not yet happened in the days of Moses. He could not have known about such things so could not have encoded them within the text. We are going to look at some of these amazing hidden messages later in this book. They are truly astonishing. They could only have come from an angelic being outside this time-space dimension.

The Dead Sea Scrolls document several extra-terrestrial encounters between Yahuah Elohim and humankind. It was during one of these extra-terrestrial encounters that the ten commandments were given. No other documents on earth can compare to the scrolls bearing the commandments.

Today the ten commandments are dismissed as inconsequential and irrelevant. This is not true as they are eternal. Nothing is more far reaching or consequential for they are the metric by which all of our lives will be measured and judged. They are the keys to eternal life.

So, if the commandments are eternal, and were written on tablets of stone, where are the tablets now? Here is a real-life mystery. Moses commissioned the construction of a golden treasure chest in which the tablets of stone were to be kept. The treasure chest is known as the Ark of the Covenant.

Bezalel and Oholiab made the Ark of the Covenant out of acacia wood and then gilded it inside and out with gold. It has a solid gold lid with two winged Cherubim angels cast in pure gold at each end, facing each other.

The solid gold lid is called the mercy seat. The Ark of the Covenant has the two tablets of stone with the ten commandments written on them inside. The Ark is somewhere on earth, but no one knows where.

A blockbuster film was released in 1981 called *'Raiders of the Lost Ark'* featuring Harrison Ford as Indiana Jones. He was an adventurer on a quest to discover the whereabouts of the lost 'Ark of the Covenant.'

Fig. 15

THE ARK OF THE COVENANT

The Ark of the Covenant is known to have supernatural power. Therefore, adventurers throughout history have sought its whereabouts. Its extraordinary power has been documented many times throughout history. When the Philistines captured it as a trophy of war from the Hebrews, the Philistine people became ill with tumours and disease. When the Ark of the Covenant was returned the Philistines recovered.

Moses' older brother Aaron became the spiritual High Priest and was appointed guardian of the Ark and the covenant. Aaron suffered personally from the devastating power of the Ark of the Covenant. Here is what happened.

Aaron had four sons. Two of them, Nadab and Abihu, entered the Holy of Holies, an inner tent where the 'Ark of the Covenant,' was kept, without observing the strict protocols beforehand. In breach of these protocols, they were consumed by a fire that came from the Ark of the Covenant. They died instantly.

When the Ark was being moved on a cart, the oxen stumbled making the Ark tilt. A man named Uzzah touched the Ark to steady it and he died instantly.

The 'Ark of the Covenant,' has unfathomable power, observed, and recorded several times by eyewitnesses throughout history. If the ten commandments do not have supernatural power, then why would Yahuah Elohim go to such efforts to protect them?

CHAPTER 5
THE DEAD SEA SCROLLS

TESTING
THE DEAD SEA SCROLLS

The Dead Sea Scrolls document the extra-terrestrial relationship between humankind and the Creator, Yahuah Elohim. They reveal secrets of the spiritual realm, the meaning of life and the history of humankind in advance.

The scrolls make many extraordinarily claims. If we are to take them seriously, we need to be sure they are credible. We are not gullible nor easily deceived, so we must test them.

Fig. 16

Dead Sea Scrolls hidden in Earthenware Jars

The authors of the scrolls tell us to 'Test everything they say and hold fast to that which is good'. Only by testing what they say will we know truth from lies. The authors tell us to take nothing at face value. Question everything which is good advice!

I ask you to challenge me too! Question everything that I say, for then you will know the truth and not be deceived. Let us now test the scrolls, but how?

Testing the scrolls is easier than you might imagine. Within the scrolls are prophecies foretelling the future. If they came true then the scrolls are credible, if they did not, then the scrolls are not credible.

Had they been written recently, there would not be much history to test. Luckily, they were written thousands of years ago so there is a lot of history we could look back on to see if they came true. If they did, then the Dead Sea Scrolls are credible. If they did not, then they are not. It is as easy as that? So, let us test them.

I have chosen a prophecy in the scroll of Daniel that we can test. It was Daniel who survived the lion's den around 600 BC, during the reign of King Nebuchadnezzar.

The king had a troubling dream where he saw a huge statue made from four types of metal; the head was of gold, the chest and arms of silver, the belly and thighs of bronze, the legs of iron and its feet partly of iron and partly of clay.

Nebuchadnezzar was alarmed to see the statue destroyed by a rock that was not cut from human hands. This infers a supernatural force. The rock became a mountain that then filled the whole world.

The king was troubled by this dream and struggled to find anyone to interpret it. Eventually, Daniel the Hebrew was summoned, and he explained to the King that each section of the statue represents a great empire yet to come.

The head of gold represents the current empire of King Nebuchadnezzar who ruled over the Babylonian Empire at that time. Daniel then prophesied the three great empires that would follow. The question is, did those three great empires follow as prophesied by Daniel? The answer is yes, they did!

After king Nebuchadnezzar came King Xerxes who ruled over the Medo-Persian Empire, followed by Alexander the Great who led the Grecian Empire, ending with the legs and feet representing the Roman Empire. The great empires that were foretold by Daniel long before they happened, came, and went exactly as he prophesied.

The two legs of the statue made from iron even represent the two halves of the Holy Roman Empire, being Rome, and Constantinople. The Roman army was the original iron legion. The prophecy came true. This gives the scroll of Daniel, found among the Dead Sea Scrolls, credibility.

There are hundreds of prophecies in the Dead Sea Scrolls foretelling great events in history, many fulfilled, others yet to be, and some being fulfilled in our lifetime. We shall test more to validate the scrolls.

The Messiah alone had over 350 prophecies foretelling His coming, His life and His death. It was prophesied who His parents would be, when and where He was to be born, what He would be called, when where and how He would die and when and where His resurrection would happen.

No mortal man could have fulfilled such prophecies about their own life, especially as the prophecies had been written hundreds of years before He was even born by several people living in different times in history and living in different countries.

Who can know when they are going to be born, or to which parents, or in which town or country? The Messiah fulfilled all these prophecies and more.

The Dead Sea Scrolls foretell the coming of the internet, worldwide pandemics, nuclear war, the dissolution of cash, a one-world banking system and a one-world government. For those who know what to look for, we can see these prophecies unfolding today, before our very eyes.

We are given prophecies to reassure us that Yahuah Elohim is in control, and we are not to fear what is to come. The scrolls are provably accurate, tested and deemed credible. Let me show you.

TESTING
THE SCROLL OF ENOCH

Fig. 17

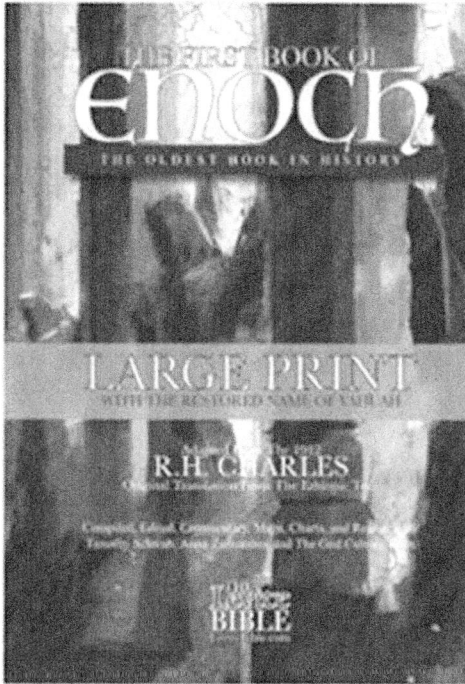

The scroll of Enoch is purported to be the first book ever written. It predates the flood in the days of Noah and reveals many secrets of creation, knowledge of the spiritual realm, the reality of angelic beings, the event around fallen angels and the truth behind demons of mental illness. It is an extraordinary book, but the question is, can the book of Enoch be trusted?

Several historical documents refer to the scroll of Enoch. Even the New Testament refers to the scroll of Enoch, his account of the fallen angels and their Nephilim offspring. This reference was made by Jude two thousand years ago. So, who was Jude? What does he know, and can we trust him?

Jude was the half-brother of the Messiah, Yahusha ha Mashiach, (Jesus the Messiah). Jude not only knew the Messiah but grew up with Him as His brother. They shared the same mother.

Jude witnessed the miracles performed by his brother. Who can have more authority or credibility on the life of Yahusha ha Mashiach, (Jesus the Messiah) than his half-brother? How can a modern scholar dispute with Jude, as Jude was there at the time and a modern scholar was not?

Who is more credible, a scholar who has only read the testimony of others or the written account of someone who was an eye-witness to these things?

Some dismiss the scroll of Enoch because it was written six thousand years ago believing Enoch to be little more than a caveman. What relevance could a six-thousand-year-old document written by a caveman have today? Enoch addresses this in his first line which says,

For the angels showed me and from them, I heard everything and from them, I understood as I saw, but not for this generation but for a remote one which is to come.

The remote generation that is to come is this generation we are living in now. We are in the last days. How do we know? The last days were described thousands of years ago as being the age of great knowledge.

We live in the information age, the age of big data. This age cannot be mistaken for any other. We are here now. This is the generation the scroll of Enoch was written for.

How strange it lay hidden, undisturbed for thousands of years and was discovered just in time for the generation for whom it is written, to read it. How mysteriously timely.

Enoch reveals the secrets of creation to prepare this generation for what is to come. He reveals knowledge we are supposed to know so we shall not fear the things we see. We are to be reassured that earth is not out of control but meticulously managed just as it has always been.

Our planet is not hurtling into oblivion with a depleted ozone layer, acid rain, excess carbon, rising sea levels, uncontrolled global warming, or pollution. These things may well be happening but are being managed by forces bigger than us overseeing every aspect of the planet.

The book of Revelation prophecies natural disasters in the last days associated with global warming. It is happening. There will be droughts, pestilence and disease, earthquakes, tsunamis, mass migrations, food shortages, wars, and rumours of wars, all the things associated with global warming and all prophesied years ago.

Yes, the planet is warming, but it was prophesied. It is meant to happen. It is happening! It was planned and we were told about it a long time ago. We are also told what we can do, but sadly science and academia pay no attention to the Creator? They mock Him at their cost.

Wind turbines, solar panels, electric cars, carbon taxes and a rushed green agenda driving millions into poverty will not stop the prophecies that have been made from being fulfilled. What has been prophesied will come to pass whatever our dithering leaders choose to do.

Drought is prophesied as are food shortages. The UK is an island, surrounded by water and known for its rainy weather, and blessed with numerous rivers that do not dry up. Yet drought will come to this land.

The UK has seen no new reservoirs for over thirty years. In that time the UK population has risen by well over ten million, all needing water. The short-sighted governments in the UK would do well to study the prophecies in the Dead Sea Scrolls, the book of Revelation or the scroll of second Ezra. It is all there!

Incompetent governments believing they can change the climate will drive millions into poverty as they and their kin take control of everything. This was prophesied in the scroll of Ezra around two thousand six hundred years ago and in the scroll of Revelation two thousand years ago.

We are to know history in advance so we will be prepared and not fear what is to come. That is the purpose of the scrolls. Creation is and always will be under strict control. How do we know this? The Angel of the Presence revealed to Enoch that we are to,

"Observe ye everything that is in the heavens, how they do not change their orbits. They rise and set in their appointed order, each in its season."

The vast moving parts of creation are set in their appointed order each according to its season. The world is not going to end any time soon as some fear but there are global changes coming.

Just because humankind is not in control of the planet does not mean the planet is not under control. It most definitely is! If humankind was in control of the planet, it would have gone to pot long ago.

Humankind does not know where the sun, moon and stars came from. We do not know how the seasons came to be or who set them in the order they are in. Science and academia do not even know how old the planet is, or where life came from, or even where it goes, yet somehow, without knowing anything of the origins of creation, humankind thinks it is in charge of planet earth. If this were not so serious, it would be funny.

Nothing on earth is random, accidental, or chaotic. The sun, moon and stars give us nights and days and the seasons of the year which are all set according to their duration and appointed order. They were put there on purpose! How else could they have got there and remained in their orbits with such precision for so long. They are set perfectly for life on earth to flourish. They are appointed and managed.

These huge moving parts and mammoth unseen forces are regulated by angelic beings under the oversight of powerful archangels. Nothing in creation evolved by itself or has self-determination. It is all regulated, planned, connected, and managed by laws, where everything has its purpose and its place. If this is not so then where did it all come from and how is it still working perfectly?

The Angel of the Presence assures us that though creation has many moving parts, it will not change, it will not wear out, fall to bits, break down, collapse or grind to a halt, despite the fears of the climate activists or environmentalists. I do not dismiss their good intentions but they do not see the bigger game at play here, for they do not see the prophecies about to be fulfilled.

Creation will not end in disaster because it is all set to perfection and meticulously managed by forces, we neither see nor hear. Just because we do not see or hear them does not mean they are not there keeping order. We know they are, because for thousands of years things have remained perfectly orderly just as we were told they would.

From the beginning there have always been 24hrs to a day, 7 days to a week, and 12 months to a year and that the year is divided into 4 seasons, all following in their appointed order and duration, all perfect for seed bearing plants to grow and animals to hibernate and procreate. The Angel of the Presence was there on the first day. He witnessed it.

He wrote it down for us so we may know these things too. Unfortunately, mainstream science considers the Archangel's account to be anti-science so discarded it as nonsense.

Creation did not evolve. We do not have to wait for any part of it to become whatever it is supposed to be. It is all here complete. Creation has never ground to a halt. It was just as it is, from the very beginning, or it would not work at all, just as we are told in the scroll of Enoch.

Now for something amazing. Enoch was shown by the Angel of the Presence how many types of evergreen trees there are in all of creation, that is globally. The results, when we test this, are mind-blowing.

In the scroll of Enoch, we read.

"Observe and see how in the winter all the trees seem as though
they have withered and shed all their leaves,
except "fourteen trees" who do not lose their
foliage but retain the old foliage from
two to three years until the new comes."

The Angel of the Presence shows Enoch fourteen types of evergreen trees worldwide, trees that do not lose their foliage in the winter. This is something we can test to see if Enoch is right.

If he is, then the Scroll of Enoch is one of the most extraordinary and mysterious books ever written. How could Enoch have had global knowledge of evergreen trees over six thousand years ago? Let us pitch Enoch against Wikipedia and see what happens.

As you will see, Wikipedia confirms and names each of the fourteen types of evergreen trees that do not shed their leaves in winter.

EVERGREEN TREES LISTED ON WIKIPEDIA

Fig. 18

No	Family Name	Example
1	Araucariaceae	Kauri
2	Cupressaceae	Sequoia
3	Pinaceae	Pine
4	Podocarpaceae	Real Yellowwood
5	Taxaceae	Yew
6	Cyatheaceae	Australian tree fern
7	Aquifoliaceae	Holly
8	Fagaceae	Live Oak
9	Oleaceae	Shamel Ash
10	Myrtaceae	Eucalyptus
11	Arecaceae	Coconut
12	Lauraceae	Bay
13	Magnoliaceae	Southern Magnolia
14	Cycadaceae	Queen Sago

Amazingly, Enoch is correct. His scroll is credible. You can read the scroll of Enoch and discover these things for yourself. See the suggested reading list at the back of this book for our preferred edition.

TESTING
THE SCROLL OF JUBILEES

Fig. 19

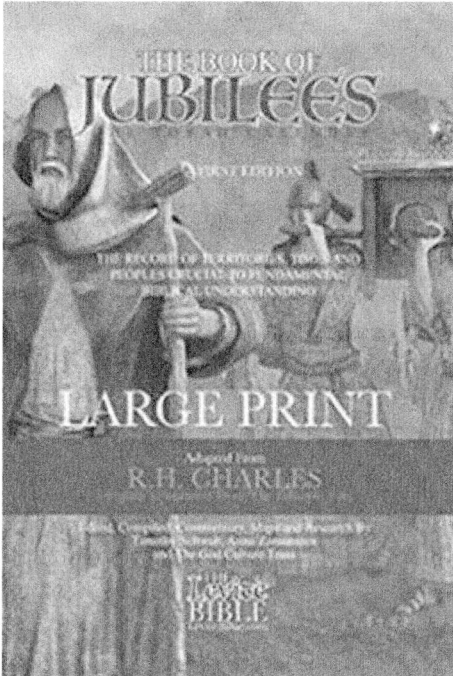

What is the scroll of Jubilees? What is a Jubilee? A jubilee is the numerical value of forty-nine. Forty-nine years is a Jubilee of years which is celebrated in the fiftieth year. The scroll of Jubilees records history from the first day of creation up to and beyond the great flood in units of jubilees, in forty-nine-year periods. That is why it is called the book of Jubilees.

Every significant historical event is recorded in its jubilee. The scroll of Jubilees is a dating system. Every generation is recorded from Adam and Eve onwards, so by this, we can know how old the earth is for it has been recorded in Jubilees from the first day of creation.

Why forty-nine-year periods? Creation took one week. That is seven-days. Seven, being a complete week is a complete unit of measure. The square of seven, as in seven sevens, make forty-nine and is known as a Jubilee. Forty-nine years is a jubilee of years. It all fits perfectly. If creation did not take one week, how is it there are still to this day, around all the world, seven days to a week? Where else could the seven-day week come from?

The scroll of Jubilees reveals the spiritual forces behind mental illness. It also reveals the art of spiritual warfare needed to overcome them. What the scroll of Jubilees says, if true, is extraordinary for it shows us how to overcome mental illness through the power of the spirit, without toxic medication. We need to test this scroll rigorously if we are to trust it. Let us test it together now.

Where did the scroll of Jubilees come from? It was written by Moses during the forty days and nights he spent with Yahuah Elohim and the Angel of the Presence on the top of Mount Sinai.

Jubilees documents and dates the many extra-terrestrial interactions between the spiritual and earthly realm. It records in detail the fall of the Watcher angels. It describes the hybrid human Nephilim, the offspring of the fallen angels who procreated with human women.

It explains how the disembodied spirits of the Nephilim become the demons behind mental illness. The scroll of Jubilees chronicles the mental health problems in Noah's family caused by demons, and how they overcame them.

As with Enoch, we test Jubilees by its prophesies. I have selected a bizarre prophecy that was given to Abraham by Yahuah Elohim, foretelling that He would become flesh and dwell among humankind as the long-awaited Messiah.

The long-prophesied Messiah will come from Abraham's descendants. The probability of such an extraordinary prophecy being fulfilled is so small that it has no meaningful mathematical value.

To compound the improbability of this prophecy, five hundred years later, the Angel of the Presence confirmed the same prophecy to Moses on top of Mount Sinai. Moses was told to write the prophecy down so humankind we may know of it well in advance.

This prophecy was given at two different times in history, to two different people living in two different countries. It would be almost two thousand years later before it came true. There is no way any man, or even group of men, could orchestrate and fulfil such an outlandish prophecy like this. Such a prophecy could only be fulfilled by forces outside this time-space dimension, as in the Creator in a spiritual realm controlling history on earth.

No one could falsely claim to be the Messiah unless He was a direct descendant of Abraham. That would certainly thin out the crazies who wanted to be a Messiah.

Abraham could not have colluded with Moses. They did not know each other. They never met. They lived in different centuries, lived in different countries, and spoke different languages.

Around two thousand years after the prophecy was given to Abraham, it came true. The Creator became flesh within Abraham's family and dwelt on earth among men. He was known as the Messiah, Yahusha ha Mashiach, (Jesus the Messiah).

The promise made to Abraham by Yahuah Elohim was fulfilled. The fulfilment of such and astonishing prophecy certainly validates the scroll of Jubilees. This is one of many extraordinary prophecies.

How do we know the Messiah was a direct descendent of Abraham? Where is the proof? Let me show you. Hebrews are fastidious about recording family trees.

I have listed this family tree so you can see who begat who from Abraham to Yahusha ha Mashiach. Before we go there let us look at the prophecy itself given to Moses by the Angel of the Presence.

It goes,

"And Abraham blessed his Creator who had created him in his generation, for He had created him according to His good pleasure: for He knew and perceived that from Him, (Abraham), would arise the plant of righteousness, (a Messiah) for the eternal generations and from him a Holy seed so that it should become like Him who had made all things, (The Creator)"

Abraham knew the Messiah would become flesh and dwell on earth, within his family. That is extraordinary by any measure of the imagination. So how do we test it?

Abraham's genealogy is recorded in the gospel of Matthew, found in the New Testament. The question is, can we trust Matthew? Matthew knew the Messiah personally. He was an eyewitness to the miracles. Matthew was an accountant, employed as a tax collector by the Roman Empire.

He was a lover of data, lists, numbers, and spreadsheets. It is not surprising it was Matthew who listed the genealogy from Abraham to the Messiah at the very beginning of his gospel. Accountants love to account.

The genealogy is tested and unchallenged. Keen for you to see the proof it is listed in the English translation, below.

"Abraham begat Yishaq begat Yacov begat Yahuda begat Phares and Zara of Thamar begat Esrom begat Aram begat Aminadab begat Naasson begat Salmon begat Booz of Rachab. Booz begat Obed begat Jesse begat David the king, (as in David and Goliath).

David the king begat Solomon begat Roboam begat Abia begat Asa begat Josaphat begat Joram begat Ozias begat Joatham begat Achaz begat Ezekias.

Ezekias begat Manasses begat Amon begat Josias begat Jechonias begat Salathiel begat Zorobabel begat Abiud begat Eliakim begat Azor begat Sadoc begat Achim begat Eliud begat Eleazar begat Matthan begat Jacob begat Joseph the husband of Mary, of whom was born 'Yahusha ha Mashiach', (Jesus the Messiah)."

What are the mathematical probabilities of that? As near to zero as is possible to get; yet there it is! The scroll of Jubilees is credible and available in English on Amazon online. Please see the recommended reading list at the back of this book for our preferred edition.

TESTING THE BIBLE

Fig. 20

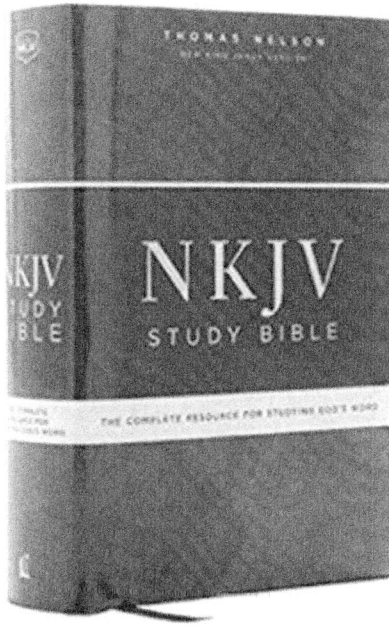

The Bible is much maligned, often by those who have never read it. Let me dispel the myths you may have heard and get to the facts. The Bible came from the Dead Sea Scrolls, so why don't we refer to the Dead Sea Scrolls as the Bible?

The Bible has been significantly edited by religion. The Dead Sea Scrolls have not. The scrolls are still in their original condition, unchanged for thousands of years. The Bible has been severely altered by Jewish and Christian religious leaders to suit their religious purposes.

Only the religious would believe they could improve on the words of the Creator. How they could believe that taking the Creator's name out was an improvement is beyond me. Entire books were removed; others added such as the Jewish book of Esther which does not mention Yahuah Elohim even once.

The discovery of the Dead Sea Scrolls in 1947 gave us back what the Bible once was and should be. For the first time in two thousand years, we could see what was missing. Reinstating the scrolls of Enoch, Jubilees and 2nd Esdras back to their rightful place within the Bible and removing other books the Jews put in, means the Bible can now be unlocked and understood.

At the end of the Bible it says,

If anyone adds to these things, Yahuah Elohim will add to him the plagues that are written in this book. If anyone takes away from the words of this book Yahuah Elohim will remove him from the 'Book of Life' kept in the heavenly realm.

Those who edited the Bible will have a lot of explaining to do on the day of judgement as will those who mock it.

Demons hate the missing scrolls being reinstated into the Bible for the scrolls make known the reality of demons and who they really are. They are exposed. The missing scrolls show us how to overcome them. This is why demons try to prevent us reading the Bible.

The Bible explains why Satan and his demons want to destroy humans. Satan and his demons once had eternal life which has now been taken from them. They know the judgement that awaits them for on that day they will perish in the lake of eternal fire.

They know eternal life awaits those who believe in Yahuah Elohim which angers them. Satan and his demons will take as many human souls with them into destruction as they can knowing each soul is a precious loss to Yahuah Elohim. For each lost soul is a lost member of Yahuah Elohim's own family.

Demons are angry because they too are part human. They had human mothers and angelic fathers but cannot become members of Yahuah's family and live forever with Him on earth but will be destroyed forever in the lake of eternal fire on the day of judgement. That is why they are specially angry toward human souls.

Many mistakenly believe the Bible belongs to religion. It does not! Nor does the Torah belong to the Jews.. They are a gift for all humankind to nourish the human spirit. They belong to all of us.

Studying them does not make us religious but spiritually wise and empowered. Spiritual empowerment leads to spiritual health through which we find eternal life. Eternal life cannot be found through religion.

The Bible is a healing balm for those in spiritual distress. It is a weapon for those under spiritual attack battling mental illness, poverty and misfortune. It is a blanket of protection from the powers of darkness that seek to harm. It is a compass to guide us through life so we may find joy, peace and abundance. It does not have a downside.

The question is, can we trust it? How can we be sure it is all the things it claims to be? We test it!

Many who have never opened a Bible before are surprised at how many familiar phrases there are. All of the following phrases come directly from the Bible.

- Fight the good fight
- A wolf in sheep's clothing
- Rise and shine
- The powers that be
- Go the extra mile
- By the skin of your teeth
- A fly in the ointment
- Give up the ghost
- The Land of Nod
- Like a lamb to the slaughter

- A millstone around your neck
- There is nothing new under the sun
- The writing is on the wall
- At the eleventh hour
- A leopard cannot change its spots
- At your wit's end
- The blind leading the blind.

No other book has shaped our language, values and laws more than the Bible. There is nothing on earth to compare it with. It has no equal. No book in history has made a bigger contribution or been more scrutinised. That is no reason why we should not test it for ourselves. Let's start by looking at the facts.

The Bible took over two thousand years to write which means it could not have been put together by a man, group of men, a religion, cult, a king, or political movement.

Another reason it is not a manmade is that it edifies the Creator, Yahuah Elohim. Not even today does man edify Yahuah Elohim, but man edifies only himself. This too proves it is not manmade.

It has at least forty authors from different countries, who lived in different times in history, speaking different languages and yet each author tells the same highly complex story of humankind's extra-terrestrial spiritual relationship with the Creator.

The Bible reveals mysteries of the spiritual realm, the art of spiritual warfare, and prophecy many great events to come. It never contradicts itself. It would be almost impossible for a modern scholar to add anything meaningful to the Bible without contradicting something already in it. So, let us test it.

The original Bible was written in Hebrew. Hebrew names have meanings. Let us take the names of the first ten generations of humankind and examine their meanings. What it reveals is truly astonishing.

Listed below are the names of the first 10 generations of humankind, which reveals a hidden sentence foretelling the fall of mankind, the coming of the Messiah and His birth, death and resurrection. It reveals the salvation of mankind on the last day of this age. It is truly astonishing!

Fig. 21. TABLE OF FIRST TEN GENERATIONS

GENERATIONS	NAME	MEANING
FIRST	ADAM	Man
SECOND	SETH	Appointed
THIRD	ENOSH	Mortal
FOURTH	KENAN	Sorrow
FIFTH	MAHALALEL	The Blessed Elohim
SIXTH	YARED	Shall Come Down
SEVENTH	ENOCH	Teaching
EIGHTH	METHUSELAH	His Death Shall Bring
NINETH	LAMECH	The Despairing
TENTH	NOAH	Rest and Comfort

The sentence hidden in the names of the first ten generations reads,

Man appointed mortal sorrow, the blessed Elohim
shall come down, teaching. His death shall
bring the despairing rest and comfort.

After Adam and Eve had been deceived they were cast out of the Garden of Eden. Life for them became far harder and for their descendants, much shorter. Being cast out of the Garden of Eden was the moment man was appointed '*mortal sorrow.*' We have been devolving ever since.

227

The blessed Elohim, as in the Messiah, Yahusha ha Mashiach, came down to earth, teaching about the commandments and eternal life. This fulfils the meanings of Mahalalel, Yared, and Enoch.

His death brings the despairing rest and comfort. This is fulfilled through the resurrection and eternal life, fulfilling the meanings of Methuselah, Lamech and Noah.

This sentence, hidden in the names of the first ten generations, is one of the hundreds of extraordinary codes and messages found in the original Hebrew Bible. Yahuah Elohim promises to put codes and secret messages in the scriptures for us to find.

If this is true, then that proves the Bible is the Word of the Creator, Yahuah Elohim, separating it from any other book on the planet. But is it true? If there are hidden messages, where else could they have come from, who else could have put them there?

The Bible even says,

"It is the glory of Yahuah Elohim to conceal a thing
but it is the honour of Kings to search
out a matter."

Yahuah delights in hiding codes and secret messages in His words as playful fun, for us to find. The bible is not meant to be dry, dusty and hard to digest but fun, playful, enlightening and empowering.

These secret messages and hidden codes are there for our joy and pleasure to seek out, and an honour for us when we find them. So, let's play, let's have some fun and go search out some of these hidden messages and see what is there.

There are many ways to decode a hidden message. One way is called 'Equidistant Letter Sequence'. This is to count letters equidistant throughout the text to reveal the hidden message. Let me give you one example that blew my socks off.

We take the first five books Moses wrote on Mount Sinai which are listed below in English and Hebrew. The five scrolls are

1. Genesis *(Bereshit),*
2. Exodus (Shemot),
3. Leviticus *(Vayikra)*
4. Numbers *(Bamidbar)*
5. Deuteronomy *(Devarim)*

We apply an equidistant letter sequence to the text. Starting from the beginning of Genesis *(Bereshit)* in the original Hebrew, and counting from the first letter 'T', we find that noting every 49 letters, (a jubilee of letters) it spells 'TORAH'.

The word 'Torah' is the Hebrew name for the first five books of the Bible. It means 'teaching law.' Did we find the word 'Torah' by chance or is this a hidden message from Yahuah Elohim? Let's test further to find out.

Looking in the scroll of Exodus, (Shemot), and applying the same sequence, again it spells 'TORAH'. Very interesting! Could this be just a coincidence? That is certainly possible, if unlikely.

Yahuah promised He would bury little surprises into the text to entertain us. These codes are there for us to find. So, let us test Leviticus, *(Vayikra)*. Unfortunately, the equidistant letter sequence does not spell 'Torah'. How disappointing. So, was it all a coincidence? Were we imagining what was never there? Quite the opposite in fact!

When we applied the equidistant letter sequence it spelt something even more extraordinary. It spelt 'YHWH', the original Hebrew spelling of Yahuah. How extraordinary is that! The true name of the Creator is embedded in the very text of Leviticus, despite religion doing all it could to remove it.

Applying this test to the book of Numbers *(Bamidbar)* it spells 'HAROT' which is Torah backwards! When we go to the book of Deuteronomy,

229

(Devarim), it also spells 'HAROT' as it did in the book of Numbers, which is Torah backwards.

Placing the codes in the order they are read, we see that the word 'Torah' points to the name of 'YHWH', the true name of the Creator. Let me show you how.

Fig. 22. HIDDEN TORAH CODE

GENESIS	EXODUS	LEVITICUS	NUMBERS	DEUTERONOMY
TORAH	TORAH	*YHWH*	HAROT	HAROT
→	→		←	←

There are hundreds of codes like this hidden in the Bible and more still to be found. Yahuah Elohim promised us little treats and surprises, and they are there in the text, just as He promised.

This gives the Bible indisputable credibility. It can only be the word of the Yahuah Elohim because it would not be possible for Moses to have put the codes in there himself. Do not forget the first five books were dictated to Moses by the Angel of the Presence on top of Mount Sinai in only forty days. The only plausible explanation is Yahuah Elohim.

Reading the Bible is not meant to be an intellectual exercise but a spiritual one. Thoughts, ideas, revelation and understanding come to mind as we read it. Certain words pop out or linger in our thoughts, giving us answers and directions to questions we may be looking for.

The Bible is spiritually interactive. It is more than a book because the words have spiritual power, for they are laws.

To purchase a bible, the edition I recommend is the New King James version which is available on Amazon online. For those wishing to study the spiritual realm further, there is a recommended home library reading list at the back of this book to help you journey deeper into the spiritual realm.

Together, we have tested the Scroll of Enoch, the Scroll of Jubilees, and the Bible. Each has proven itself to be credible. This means they can be trusted when used in spiritual warfare to restore the health of the spirit.

The scrolls of Enoch, Jubilees and the Bible are weapons of spiritual warfare. They are now tested, locked and loaded. The next question is are we ready to go into battle? Are we ready to bring down the demons of mental illness? I say we are, so let's advance on the enemy together.

CHAPTER 6
SPIRITUAL WARFARE

THE POWER OF THOUGHTS, WORDS AND BELIEFS

Spiritual warfare is an unseen conflict happening right now in the spiritual realm. It is swirling around us all the time. Lawful forces from the heavenly realm are in constant conflict with lawless forces from the satanic realm.

The friction created by this conflict spills into our lives in many forms. Lawful energy spills over as healing, good fortune, opportunity, joy, happiness, loving relationships, empathy, trust, courage, kindness, patience and abundance. These outcomes are when lawful forces dominate the conflict.

Lawless forces spill over into our lives as mental illness, chronic sickness, poverty, infertility, toxic relationships, violence, abuse, suicide misfortune, sadness, loneliness, rejection, guilt, shame, lack of confidence, self-harm, eating disorders, and more besides. These outcomes are when lawless forces become dominant in our life.

The ebb and flow of those forces is regulated by the quality of the thoughts, words and beliefs we choose to dwell on. Dwelling on positive thoughts, words and beliefs strengthens lawful outcomes whereas dwelling on negative thoughts, words and beliefs strengthen lawless outcomes.

We can control these unseen forces by regulating the quality of our thoughts, words and beliefs. Regulating the quality of our thoughts with skill and purpose is the art of spiritual warfare. When we feel negative thoughts coming into our mind we can consciously push back with positive thoughts. This is discernment, a fruit of the spirit.

The weapons of spiritual warfare are positive thoughts, words and beliefs for the enemy is in our thoughts, words and beliefs. Spiritual warfare is about using positive thoughts, words and beliefs to overcome negative ones. Thoughts, words and beliefs have immense power that is very much overlooked.

Spiritual warfare teaches discernment between lawful thoughts, words and beliefs from lawless. Discernment transforms our quality of life, overcoming mental health and restoring the spirit. Let me show you how it works.

Someone wrongs you. What do you do? The carnal-self is always quick to respond seeking to take revenge. Revenge is a trap for it is always negative. Someone wrongs you, have discernment. Quell the carnal self for a moment and take a breath. Stand back and let the situation play out.

Let me show you what I mean. We are looking for a parking space in a crowded hospital carpark. Finally we see a space. Just as we go to park in it another car whizzes in. A man jumps out and rushes off.

How easy is it for our carnal self to get angry and feel wronged. What we didn't see was that the man had had just received a phone call to say his wife and baby had been in an accident and both were critically ill and had been rushed to the hospital. Do we feel as angry with him, now that we know this. See how it changes everything.

Our boss at work treats us unfairly. How easy it is to get angry with him? What if he has just found out his partner has been unfaithful? Or he had test results showing a serious illness, or his house is about to be repossessed. His unfairness toward you was not about you at all.

It is all too easy to be angry with someone before we know what is truly going on. Spiritually wise people will stand back and let the situation play out because things are seldom as they seem. As the saying goes, best not to sing before the hymn is given out.

Yahuah Elohim sees everything. Let Him take revenge on your behalf for it is written,

'vengeance is mine says Yahuah Elohim.'

He would not tell us vengeance is His if He was not going to take vengeance on our behalf.

Knowledge is the root to belief. Positive belief grows with knowledge and empowers and heals the spirit. Negative belief can also grow with negative knowledge and ignorance for it too empowers the spirit, but with dark energy that brings poor health and misfortune. All beliefs have energy as do all thoughts and all words. We need to discern positive from negative before we think, believe and speak because we will reap what we s ow.

This is constant conflict between lawful and lawless energy. There is a quick way to feel this conflict for yourself.

Close your eyes and imagine being at the beach on a hot summer's day. You are sweltering and your throat is dry. You are given an ice cream. It is cool, refreshing and soft on the tongue. It is delicious. Keep your eyes closed and imagine it. Hold that thought. Dwell on it for a few moments. Enjoy it.

Now open your eyes and think immediately of something sad. Not easy, is it? Did you feel the tension between a happy thought and a sad one? There is resistance between a happy thought and a sad one because they can't both exist in our head at the same time. This is the friction between positive and negative energy and the foundation of spiritual warfare.

Positive thoughts bare fruits of the spirit. Dwelling on positive thoughts protects the fruit because we can't think of positive and negative thoughts at the same time, as we proved with our ice-cream experiment.

Mental illness is negative energy which shuts positive energy out. We need to make a conscious effort to focus on the positive. The ten commandments give us the strength and direction to think of positive thoughts we would not find on our own. When our mind is deep in negative territory the commandments will guide us back into positive territory.

The power of the spoken word is known as the sword of the spirit. The sword of the spirit is to speak spiritual laws aloud. When Yahuah Elohim's spirit, the Ruach ha Kodesh, dwells within ours, and we speak aloud the laws, it is as if He were speaking the laws through us. They are immensely powerful and can even change the physical world around us.

Using thoughts, beliefs and the power of the spoken word in a single purpose, we can access power to drive the spiritual forces behind mental illness out. I will show how to do this, step by step. It is easier than you think and far more powerful than you might imagine.

How can the spoken word have power over the spiritual forces behind mental illness? Surely spoken words are just words. What power does a spoken word have?

Spiritual pathogens behind mental illness were once part human. Rebuke them with powerful laws spoken aloud and they respond emotionally just as humans do. They can be driven out by fear. Spoken words are more than just words. They have power. Let me show you.

Many who are oblivious to the power of the spoken word hurt and upset people by what they say leaving a trail of emotional carnage behind them. Only when they are verbally threatened or chastised themselves do they appreciate the power of the spoken word.

Angry words can make us feel frightened, sick, or angry in return. We either freeze, flee or fight back. This is the power of the spoken word.

Blackmail has the power to force someone to part with all they have or even commit murder or suicide. That is the power of the spoken word.

The pain of rejection from someone you love, making you feel sick to your stomach for weeks on end, is the power of the spoken word.

The hurt that comes from words of betrayal by someone you trusted is the power of the spoken word.

The sting of public humiliation is the power of the spoken word.

The calming affect of a mother's gentle words to her baby is the power of the spoken word.

The relief of a friend standing by you in a time of crisis is the power of the spoken word.

Encouragement when we just can't go on is the power of the spoken word.

Being forgiven is the power of the spoken word.

Reconciliation is the power of the spoken word.

Hostage negotiation is the power of the spoken word.

The spoken word has immense unseen power. The spiritual entities behind mental illness react to the spoken word just as we do for they are part human and have emotions. They had human mothers. They are emotionally driven which is why they seek vengeance on us.

They feed off negative emotion which can be generated through the spoken word. They react emotionally to the spoken word just as you and I do. Many ancient proverbs allude to the power of the spoken word. These proverbs are thousands of years old and come from the Dead Sea Scrolls.

*"A kindly word turns away wrath,
but a harsh word stirs up anger."*

*"Gentle words bring life and health.
a deceitful tongue crushes the spirit."*

*"Kind words are like honey-sweet to the soul
and healthy for the body."*

*"Your soul is nourished when you are kind,
but you destroy also yourself when you are cruel."*

*"Wise speech is rarer and more valuable
than gold and rubies."*

*"Like being cut with a sword or pierced by an arrow
is one who lies about his neighbour."*

*"It is not what goes into a man's mouth that makes
him unclean but what comes out."*

Even if you are alone in a room, the spoken word still has power because it is heard in the spiritual realm by angelic beings, Yahuah Elohim and demons, as in familiar spirits. I am going to show you how to harness and direct this power against the demons of mental illness, with devastating effect.

You have the power to take down demonic strongholds even if you are alone in a room. You have the power to retake lost territories of the mind. No longer are you going to be held back. Do not be afraid to use this power.

Before we release this immense power, let us have a quick look at one form of negative spiritual energy that is not mental illness but has a category of its own. I am talking about curses. Curses impair spiritual health yet are mostly overlooked. Spiritual health also overcomes curses.

Curses are more common than many realize. Let me explain what they are in the next section and then we will be ready to start healing using the art of spiritual warfare.

CURSES

Few today have any idea of what a curse is. Curses are routinely dismissed as fanciful myths or inventions of the past, yet I can prove that curses are real and more common than is realised.

Curses are negative forces that adversely impact our lives. They are negative beliefs we hold about ourselves, the world around us, and are usually untrue, disproportionate or irrational, but that does not stop us from believing them.

Curses hold us back. They prevent us from reaching our full potential and prospering. They are called irrational beliefs, fears or phobias. They are a curse on life and stop us from being all we can be.

Curses or irrational beliefs, fears, or phobias are rooted in the spirit. Confidence, for example is a fruit of the spirit. When confidence is gone it is often replaced with an irrational fear of the world around us hindering our potential. That is a curse.

An irrational belief would be to believe we are less able than others so why even bother to try. That is a curse that holds us back. Irrational or untrue negative beliefs in our character preventing us from reaching our destiny in life can be seen as a curse.

There are hundreds of different types of curses just as there are hundreds of different types of irrational beliefs, fears, phobias. Curses lead people to say things like, I must put everyone else first so I am not seen as selfish or, I am fat, I am ugly, no one loves me, I am terrified of flying, I will never be successful, I am not creative, I am shy, I have no confidence, I am no good at sports and I can't do maths.

Almost always, curses have been cast by the power of the spoken word. Let me show you how easily this can happen.

A student struggling with maths is told by a frustrated teacher, "You can't do maths, you just don't get it do you?" The student is frustrated and confused so accepts the authority of the spoken word from their teacher. What the teacher said must be true because they are the teacher so they must know. The power of the spoken word then becomes reality. The curse has been cast by the power of the spoken word.

Being unable to do maths is now embedded in their subconscious, in their spirit, as a belief. It is an untrue negative belief that has now become reality, a curse that will hold them back for the rest of their life, or until the curse is broken.

This poor soul may have an opportunity to do the perfect job for them, to do what they are born to do, but if there is a hint of maths, the curse will kick in and they will avoid it, missing their perfect opportunity. That is a curse.

People attend my studio with a deep longing to draw but are convinced they can't. Sometime in the past someone was critical of their work and the power of the spoken word destroyed their self-belief, confidence and creativity, all fruits of the spirit. They never drew again despite a deep longing in their soul to draw. That curse told them they couldn't. That was the power the curse had over them, until it was broken.

I would like to share a true story of a curse over someone I knew who had a great talent. This person was robbed of a successful career as an artist, because of a curse unknowingly cast by the power of the spoken word.

It began when a mature student attended my art studio for private tuition. She was in her late sixties and came from high society. Secretly, she had dreamt of going to art school since childhood but was denied the opportunity.

Young ladies of her social position were supposed to devote their efforts and attention to husbands and family, and to patronising charitable organisations, and not becoming an art student.

Elders in her family deemed art a frivolous indulgence enjoyed by children. It was not an option for a lady of her position. The power of those words forced her to abandon her art materials despite having an amazing talent and a deep longing to draw and paint. She had been unknowingly cursed.

Throughout life her talent was concealed for fear of being seen as self-indulgent, frivolous and neglecting her social duties. Finally, when her husband retired, she enrolled at my art studio and began a formal education as a fine art painter.

From day one it was apparent to everyone in the studio that she had an incredible talent. The gift she had was extraordinary. When she was at the easel she glowed with joy and produced extraordinary works of art, one after the other, day after day.

Within weeks we submitted her work for an exhibition. It was her first art exhibition. She won the gold medal. Finally, she was living the life she had longed for. She was doing what she knew she was destined to do, and now she had the life she had always wanted. The curse had been broken; it was now time to live! Or so we thought!

Within a year she was diagnosed with cancer. By the following year, she had passed away. We were all devastated. The curse that told her she should not draw and paint because it would be selfish and frivolous had robbed her of her destiny as an extraordinary artist. I have no doubt, had she not been cursed, she would have produced the highest quality art of her generation.

You may say, well, she was probably happy tending her family and patronising charities. She was not unhappy, that I know, but unfulfilled. When I spoke to her family at the funeral, none of them had any idea she could draw before she attended my studio. No idea at all.

Many family members said that if they had known of her longing to go to art school and the incredible talent she so obviously had, they would have supported her all the way. They would have been so proud of her. With that level of talent, she would have been very successful and highly esteemed in both the world of art and her family. She never knew how supportive the family were.

That negative belief in her head was a curse that held her back, and when the curse was broken, sadly, it came too late. Curses rob people of the fruit of the spirit, their talents and their true destiny. We have been given fruits of the spirit and talents to fulfil our destiny. Anything that hinders that is a curse.

Curses come in many forms. They can affect entire families for generations. Poverty, misfortune, divorce, infertility, mental health issues, suicide, accidents, and premature death, are all typical outcomes from curses that run through entire families.

Familiar curses are like familiar spirits and operate within familiar territories. That familiar territory may be a family, a social group, a corporation, or even an entire town. Ships are said to have curses as are coal mines and factories. Curses thrive wherever there are collections of souls.

The power of a curse is in the spoken word, because it influences what we think and believe. That is why it is written that,

What you think about you bring about. Whether you think you can or whether you think you can't, either way, you will probably be right!

There is power in our thoughts, our beliefs and our spoken words. Positive thoughts, beliefs and words bring healing and abundance, negative thoughts and words can bring curses.

I will share in the next section powerful scripts, thousands of years old, that have immense spiritual power. They can overcome curses and demons. They unlock the hidden power within the ten commandments, the power of the Ruach ha Kodesh that dwells within us.

It is by this power we are healed, and lives are transformed. So let us have a look at these spiritually weaponised scripts that are known as the, *'Sword of the Spirit'*.

THE SWORD
OF THE SPIRIT IN SCRIPTS

Below are powerful scripts for spiritual warfare that date back six thousand years to the days of Enoch. They are meticulously structured and have immense power, if used in faith. They have the power to drive out demons, bring healing, peace, joy and abundance.

These words, originally in Hebrew, were used by Abraham over four thousand years ago and by Moses three thousand seven hundred years ago. They were used by Noah, Ezra, and Ezekiel. We shall use them too. We are in good company.

Demons cannot stand these scripts because they are the words of Yahuah Elohim. They are His laws. Because His spirit dwells within us, it is as if He is speaking His words to the demons through us.

The second principle of spiritual warfare is to know yourself. Restoring your spirit is to know yourself. The 'Art of War', by Sun Tzu says,

"When you know the enemy and know yourself, you will never be in peril. To know only one or the other is to be equal to the enemy. To be ignorant of both brings the certainty of losing every battle."

Do not take these scripts lightly or use then carelessly. Be mindful of them. They have real power. Others have ridiculed them and, in their jests, brought down curses upon themselves. They are the sword of the spirit and nothing in creation is spiritually sharper. In the scroll of Hebrews is says.

For the word of Yahuah is alive and active. Sharper than any double-edged sword, it penetrates even to dividing soul and spirit, joints and marrow; it judges the thoughts and attitudes of the heart.

These scripts can separate demons from souls. So, handle with care. The first script comes from the tablets of stone written by the Creator on Mount Sinai. They are eternal laws. They have power and authority over every living creature on earth, even demons. Demons know these laws and fear them.

Printable versions can be found at www.rosaleetuffney.com. Do not be self-conscious when you read them aloud. Demons will try and make you feel embarrassed because they fear the power within those scripts. Those scripts give you immense power and authority over them.

These words have been used throughout history. They have endured for thousands of years. Now it is your turn to use them. You are not the first nor the last to take the sword of the spirit from its scabbard and use it against the powers of darkness. Do not be self-conscious. Be determined and ferocious in your confidence and belief.

When you are healed, and others see what you have achieved, they will want you to share with them this immense power hidden in your spirit. Share these things with everyone for they are a gift for us all.

Do not forget that the Creator is omniscient, all knowing, He hears you as do the angels. You may think you are alone, but you are not. Even if there is nobody else in the room with you, your words are still heard in the spiritual realm.

We are now ready to confront the demons of mental illness. Find somewhere quiet, safe and warm where you will not be disturbed for around twenty minutes. Get comfortable with cushions or a blanket. Do not lie down for fear of falling asleep but sit upright and relax.

Avoid background music because that can be distracting. Incense, perfume or fresh flowers have positive energy and can help. Enjoy the peace and quiet as we begin.

PROTECTION UNDER THE LAW

(Recite Aloud)

I BELIEVE IN YAHUAH ELOHIM. I BELIEVE HE IS THE
CREATOR OF HEAVEN AND EARTH. I SHALL NOT
BOW DOWN AND WORSHIP ANY IMAGE IN THE
FORM OF ANYTHING IN HEAVEN ABOVE,
OR ON EARTH BENEATH OR IN THE
WATERS BELOW.

I SHALL NOT MISUSE THE NAME OF YAHUAH ELOHIM
OR HIS SON, YAHUSHA HA MASHIACH.

I WILL KEEP THE SABBATH.
FOR SIX DAYS I SHALL LABOUR AND DO ALL MY WORK,
BUT ON THE SEVENTH DAY I SHALL DO NO WORK.

(Pause so the words can release their power)

I WILL HONOUR MY FATHER AND MOTHER, SO THAT I MAY
LIVE LONG IN THE LAND I HAVE BEEN GIVEN.
I SHALL NOT COMMIT MURDER,
I SHALL NOT COMMIT ADULTERY,
I SHALL NOT STEAL.

(Pause to let the words release their power)

I SHALL NOT GIVE FALSE TESTIMONY
AGAINST MY NEIGHBOUR!

I SHALL NOT COVET MY NEIGHBOUR, NOR HIS HOUSE,
NOR HIS SPOUSE NOR ANYTHING THAT BELONGS
TO MY NEIGHBOUR.

YAHUSHA HA MASHIACH SAID, IF YOU LOVE ME, KEEP MY
COMMANDMENTS. I KEEP HIS COMMANDMENTS
FOR I LOVE HIM AS HE LOVES ME.

I DELIGHT IN HIS LAWS, I AM PROTECTED BY THEM,
THE RUACH HA KODESH DWELLS WITHIN MY SOUL.
I AM IN COVENANT WITH YAHUAH ELOHIM,
I BELONG TO HIM.

(Pause so the words may release their power)

END OF SCRIPT 1

Sit quietly and allow the words to release their power. You may feel a tingle. This is relief in the spirit. Repeat as often as you are led by your spirit. You cannot say these words too often, for they generate huge amounts of positive energy, bringing protection to you and panic to the demons.

Frequently Asked Questions
About Script No 1.

What if I no longer have parents?
If parents have passed away, honour their memory. Speak well of them. Do not speak ill of them even if they were neglectful or unkind because that is a trap. Better to say nothing than dishonour their memory. Recite the script even if your parents are now resting in peace, in Sheol.

How can I keep the Sabbath if I have work commitments?
If current employment requires working on Saturdays, do not fret. Yahuah Elohim knows everything. He sees your situation. Ask Him to make the Sabbath possible. Make your request known. Speak from the heart and know He hears you. You will see your life change in unexpected ways. Recite the script even if you work on Shabbat for in your heart you want to keep it.

What if I have been convicted of stealing, murder, fraud or perjury?
When you keep the spiritual laws of life you become a new creation. What happened in the past is gone. You are not going to steal, commit fraud, murder or perjure yourself again because you no longer belong to the world but to Yahuah Elohim. You have been given a fresh start. Enjoy it.

In time Yahuah Elohim will show you how to confess and repent of things for which you need to be forgiven. This removes lawlessness that may linger from the past. When He forgives us, we must remember to forgive ourselves. If we continue to feel guilty and ashamed after Yahuah Elohim has forgiven us, then we have not forgiven ourselves.

Guilt and shame invite demons, giving them negative energy to feed off. There is no condemnation in Yahusha ha Mashiach. If He can forgive you, so can you!

What if I had an abortion?

We cannot undo the past. Abortion is to take a life. Life is not ours to take. If we have taken a life we can seek forgiveness for taking what did not belong to us. All life comes from the Creator. All life belongs to Him. Therefore, it is to Him we owe the debt and from Him, we need to be forgiven.

Pro-choice activists know nothing of the spiritual realm, for if they did, they would not hold the views they do. Neither do they know anything of the judgement of the soul. They are blind guides leading many to destruction. Follow them at your peril.

We all have free will. You can choose to repent as soon as right now, if you want. Following repentance comes forgiveness. Nothing is beyond the forgiveness of Yahuah Elohim. Not even murder.

Remember, the pro-choice activists will not be there in your defence when you are judged. Repentant souls atone for the lawless things they have done and are forgiven. Repentance is between you and the Creator. He will wait your entire life for you to come to Him in repentance. He waits for all of us because we have all broken the commandments and done stupid things. None of us are perfect.

Let us support each other to do the best we can at keeping the spiritual laws of life. None of us is blameless, nor ever will be. That is why we need forgiveness and grace. We also need support and love from each other. The Yahudim are known to the world by their love for one another.

Because we all make mistakes, and always will, we cannot earn eternal life. Because we all fall short of righteousness, none of us would qualify. Eternal life is given to us as a gift by Yahuah Elohim just as our life is.

It is by His grace on our day of judgement that we receive eternal life. It is not something we can earn or buy but is promised to those who believe in Him and keep His commandments. It is that simple.

SCRIPT 2

ASSERTING AUTHORITY
OVER DEMONS

(Recite Aloud)

I BELIEVE IN YAHUAH ELOHIM. THIS GIVES ME SPIRITUAL POWER AND AUTHORITY OVER DEMONS, OVER MENTAL ILLNESS, AND PHYSICAL SICKNESS. I REBUKE ALL UNCLEAN SPIRITS THAT HAVE TORMENTED ME.

THE SPIRIT OF YAHUAH ELOHIM, THE RUACH HA KODESH, DWELLS WITHIN ME. IT IS WRITTEN, HE WHO IS IN ME IS GREATER THAN HE WHO IS IN THE WORLD.

THE UNCLEAN SPIRITS THAT TORMENT ME BELONG TO SATAN, PRINCE OF THIS WORLD. SATAN IS THE FATHER OF LIES. YOU SEEK THE DESIRES OF YOUR FATHER FOR HE WAS A MURDERER FROM THE BEGINNING.

NEITHER HE NOR YOU CAN STAND IN TRUTH FOR THERE IS NO TRUTH IN YOU OR HIM. I AM IN THIS WORLD BUT NOT OF IT. I STAND IN THE TRUTH SO YOU CANNOT STAND AGANST ME

HE WHO DWELLS WITHIN ME HAS POWER AND AUTHORITY OVER SATAN AND ALL HIS DEMONS. IT IS BY HIS AUTHORITY I HAVE POWER OVER ALL DEMONS.

(Pause so the words can release their power)

*I COMMAND ALL UNCLEAN SPIRITS THAT TORMENT ME TO
LEAVE MY SOUL RIGHT NOW! NO UNCLEAN SPIRIT HAS
ANY PLACE HERE. UNCLEAN SPIRITS HAVE NO
AUTHORITY OVER ME. GO NOW IN THE
NAME OF YAHUSHA HA MASHIACH.*

*MY SOUL IS REDEEMED, BOUGHT AND PAID FOR BY THE
BLOOD OF YAHUSHA HA MASHIACH. I AM HIS,
THEREFORE MY SOUL IS SANCTIFIED BY HIS BLOOD.*

*UNCLEAN SPIRITS HAVE NO LAWFUL PLACE HERE.
I COMMAND YOU TO GO NOW AND DO NOT RETURN.*

(Pause so the words may release their power)

END OF SCRIPT TWO
Stay quiet for around 20 seconds to give the demons time to leave. They cannot leave while you are speaking. As they depart you may feel a lifting of the spirit, dizziness, tearfulness or relief. Repeat often to reinforce your power and authority. With each repetition you are causing fear and panic among the powers of darkness. They will go.

EVICTING UNCLEAN SPIRITS

(Recite Aloud)

I REBUKE ALL SATANIC FORCES. I EVICT ALL DEMONS OF MENTAL ILLNESS. I HAVE THE POWER TO EVICT FOR I SPEAK ON THE AUTHORITY OF THE LAWS OF YAHUAH ELOHIM.

BY THOSE LAWS, I CAST YOU UNCLEAN SPIRITS THAT TORMENT ME, OUT, FOR YOU HAVE NO LAWFUL RIGHT TO BE HERE. I COMMAND YOU TO GO NOW!

(Pause to allow the demons to leave.)

I AM SPEAKING TO YOU UNCLEAN SPIRITS. I KNOW WHO YOU ARE, I KNOW WHAT YOU ARE. I KNOW WHERE YOU ARE FROM. I KNOW WHERE YOU ARE DESTINED. I KNOW YOU CAN NOT TOLERATE THE LAWS OF YAHUAH ELOHIM. I HAVE PROTECTION UNDER OF THOSE LAWS.

I KNOW YOU HEAR ME, UNCLEAN SPIRITS OF THE NEPHILIM. YOU HOWLERS AND YELPERS WHO LEAD ASTRAY THE SOULS OF MAN AND TAKE AWAY THE SPIRIT OF UNDERSTANDING.

I COMMAND YOU TO LEAVE RIGHT NOW. I BREAK THE CHAINS THAT BIND ME. I BREAK FREE FROM YOU RIGHT NOW, FOR YOU NO LONGER HAVE ANY AUTHORITY OVER ME, NOR ANY LAWFUL RIGHT TO BE HERE.

(Stay quiet for 20 seconds or so to allow the demons to leave.)

IT IS WRITTEN THOSE WHO BELIEVE IN YAHUSHA HA MASHIACH WILL DO WHAT HE HAS DONE, AND EVEN GREATER THINGS THAN THESE. I BELIEVE, WHICH MEANS I TOO WILL DO THESE THINGS THAT ARE WRITTEN. I TOO HAVE THE POWER TO CAST OUT DEMONS.

YAHUSHA HA MASHIACH SAID THAT HE WILL DO WHATEVER I ASK IN HIS NAME, SO HE MAY BRING GLORY TO HIS FATHER IN HEAVEN, YAHUAH ELOHIM. THAT I MAY ASK HIM FOR ANYTHING IN HIS NAME AND HE WILL DO IT!

I ASK IN HIS NAME, THAT ALL UNCLEAN SPIRITS OF MENTAL ILLNESS THAT TORMENT ME, BE CAST OUT. THAT I WILL BE HEALED. IT IS WRITTEN THAT YOU WILL GIVE ME A SPIRIT OF COURAGE AND OF A SOUND MIND.

IN HIS HOLY NAME, YAHUAH ELOHIM AND THE NAME OF HIS SON, YAHUSHA HA MASHIACH. ALLELUIA. AMEN

(Pause for around 20 seconds to release the power of the words)

SCRIPT 4

BREAKING CURSES

(Recite Aloud)

I REBUKE ALL CURSES THAT HAVE BOUND ME. I BREAK EVERY CURSE THAT HAS POWER OVER ME. I CRUSH ALL CURSES THAT HAVE EVER HELD ME BACK.

THE LAW SAYS NO WEAPON FORMED AGAINST ME WILL PREVAIL. CURSES ARE WEAPONS. I BREAK ALL CURSES AGAINST ME FOR THE LAW STATES THEY CANNOT PREVAIL BEFORE THE LAW. I KEEP HIS LAWS AND CLAIM THEIR AUTHORITY AND PROTECTION.

I RENOUNCE ALL CONTACT WITH THE OCCULT, WITCHCRAFT, AND DIVINATION, I RENOUNCE ALL CONTACT WITH CLAIRVOYANCE AND SPIRITUALISM. FROM THIS MOMENT I WILL STAY AWAY FROM ALL THE POWERS OF DARKNESS.

I REJECT AND REBUKE ALL SATANIC POWERS. I BREAK ALL AND EVERY HOLD THEY HAVE OVER ME. NO LONGER WILL THEY HAVE ANY POWER OVER MY LIFE.

(Pause so the words can release their power)

I BREAK ALL CURSES OVER MY FAMILY, I BREAK ALL CURSES THAT HAVE COME FROM MY ANCESTORS, OR THROUGH CONTACT WITH THE OCCULT.

I REBUKE AND BREAK THEM ALL RIGHT NOW. YAHUAH ELOHIM DID NOT GIVE ME A SPIRIT OF FEAR BUT OF POWER, AND OF LOVE, AND OF A SOUND MIND.

I CLAIM THESE SPIRITUAL POWERS THAT I HAVE BEEN PROMISED, IN THE NAME OF YAHUAH ELOHIM. AMEN.

(Pause so the words can release their power)

SCRIPT 5

GIVING THANKS

(Recite Aloud)

THANK YOU YAHUAH ELOHIM FOR CALLING ME,
THANK YOU FOR REVEALING YOURSELF TO ME.
THANK YOU FOR BEING THERE AND FOR THE
POWER TO SELF-HEAL AND TO HEAL OTHERS.

THANK YOU FOR GIVING ME POWER AND AUTHORITY
OVER DEMONS, THANK YOU FOR GIVING ME THE POWER
TO BREAK CURSES. THANK YOU FOR REVEALING YOUR
LAWS TO ME. THANK YOU FOR THE PROTECTION
YOUR LAWS GIVE ME.

THANK YOU FOR THE MYSTERY OF THE CROSS. I KNOW
YOU WERE PUNISHED FOR MY SINS. I KNOW YOU
WERE PIERCED FOR MY TRANSGRESSIONS AND
CRUSHED FOR MY INIQUITIES. THE PUNISHMENT
THAT BROUGHT ME PEACE WAS ON YOU. BY YOUR
WOUNDS I AM HEALED.

(Pause so your thanks can be heard)

FORGIVE ME FOR ALL THE TIMES I HAVE BROKEN YOUR LAWS. FORGIVE ME FOR ANYTHING I HAVE DONE THAT IS STOPPING ME FROM EVICTING UNCLEAN SPIRITS.

FORGIVE ME FOR ANYTHING I HAVE DONE THAT IS STOPPING ME FROM SELF-HEALING OR HEALING OTHERS. FORGIVE ME FOR ANYTHING I HAVE DONE THAT IS STOPPING ME FROM BREAKING CURSES OVER MY LIFE, AND OVER THE LIVES OF OTHERS.

GUIDE AND PROTECT ME SO I MAY CONTINUE TO LIVE AND GROW IN COVENANT WITH YOU. THANK YOU, HEAVENLY FATHER. ALLELUIA. AMEN.

(Pause so your thanks can be heard)

Printable scripts can be downloaded from our website at:
www.rosaleetuffney.com

CHAPTER 7
KEEPING DEMONS OUT

DON'T GIVE UP

Do not give up! Demons behind mental illness never want to leave and will do all they can to remain. They will tempt you with thoughts and beliefs that directly contradict what you have learnt in this book. They know that what you have learnt gives you the power and authority to overcome them. You have the power, so do not be afraid to use it.

These scripts have been used successfully for thousands of years. They were given to us by Yahuah Himself. Demons know this and they also know every word in them. Say these powerful scripts aloud whenever you are under attack or seeking spiritual protection. They have the power to protect, to heal, to restore the health of your spirit and set you on the path you were born to live because we are born to thrive and succeed.

By deepening belief, wisdom and understanding you will see healing of the mind and the spirit. The changes may be immediate and dramatic or slow and gentle. Let your healing be whatever it is meant to be.

Persistence is key! There are many examples in the Dead Sea Scrolls where persistence won the day. Those who give up are sure of only one thing, defeat! In Jubilees we read of Abram's persistence against hordes of demons in the form of ravens.

They appeared as great clouds and drove his community into destitution by eating all the seeds of their crops before they could take root and grow. The hordes of ravens ate all the fruit of the trees before they could be harvested leaving the community continuously hungry and impoverished.

Abram used the same spiritual warfare to drive out the hordes of ravens we use today. He used the sword of the spirit just as I have shown you with these scripts. You can read for yourself in Jubilees how He spoke aloud the laws of Yahuah Elohim and drove them away sixty-nine times and each time they returned. Only on the seventieth time did they go and not return. That is persistence!

What if Abram had only driven them away 69 times and gone home saying this stuff doesn't work? Only after commanding the ravens to leave seventy times did the ravens finally go and not return. That is persistence!

We shall do the same and persist until we win. Every time these scripts are recited they chip away at demonic strongholds in the mind. Eventually those demonic strongholds fall.

It took me years to learn spiritual warfare and break free from demons. I now help others break free in weeks. Some recoveries are sudden and dramatic. Others are slow and gentle. Allow your recovery to be what it is meant to be.

Give your recovery the time it needs. We all recover differently. Just as some seeds take longer than others to germinate, so it is with our recovery. Some healings take more time than others. Moses went into the wilderness for forty years after killing the Egyptian overseer. That was a long slow recovery, but what a life he lived after that.

My recovery was slow, but I stuck with it because I knew there was nowhere else to go. There is only one maker of my spirit. Restoring your spirit will transform your life and bring you wonderful blessings. Be patient, be persistent, and allow the Creator time to give you all the blessings He has for you. It will be worth it. Your life will never be the same again.

WHAT IF DEMONS
DON'T GO?

If the demons of mental illness don't go, there will be a reason. You have the power, and the authority so there must be a point of law that is being overlooked. Demons know a lot about you and may have been with you from childhood. They may be using lawless events you have forgotten because you were too young to know or understand what was happening.

Familiar spirits can attach themselves to people and families for an entire lifetime. This means they are familiar with every detail of a soul's life and their family, from a very young age.

My demons of violence and sexual abuse went back to when I was too young to understand what was happening. I could not do anything about the things being done to me but that did not stop the lawless energy and the demons attaching themselves to me.

Demons tormented me for many years. I could not stop them. I could not get rid of them until I had dealt with the negative energy that allowed them in. That is what took years for me to understand and overcome.

Lawlessness needs to be confessed aloud to Yahuah Elohim. When confessed, He will forgive and that washes the lawless energy away leaving nothing for the demons to feed off or cling to. They lose their right to stay and must go. Then there is healing.

If demons still won't go, turn to the Creator. Ask for a revelation. Ask for the wisdom and understanding you need to break free. It may be a curse passed down from your ancestors that needs to be broken. Ask to be shown what needs to be done.

There are certain demons that will only come forth by prayer and fasting. I will be covering these skills on my YouTube channel. You may wish to learn more there.

Whatever problems you might face overcoming demons behind mental illness, know that Yahuah Elohim knows the solution for He is omniscient, all knowing.

He hears you for He dwells in your spirit. He will answer you. The answer will come through your intuition, insight, thoughts, ideas and dreams. This is how we hear Yahuah Elohim. Our spiritual relationship with Him is two-way and is very real.

SPEAKING
TO YAHUAH ELOHIM

We can speak to Yahuah in the full assurance that He hears. This practice was once called prayer and was common. Today, few people even believe there is a Creator, let alone bother to speak or listen to Him.

Speaking to Yahuah Elohim is not difficult. There is no ritual or ceremony. Just speak plainly and let it come straight from the heart. Whatever you say in faith is heard. To make your prayers and petitions more powerful there are some basic principles we use. They are listed below.

BE HONEST.
Be yourself and speak from the heart. Yahuah Elohim is not big on feigned eloquence or fancy words. He knows all the big words in every language and will not be impressed.

Do not give a performance or try to entertain. He gets enough of that from the religious. He is looking for honesty. Do not read from scripts (we use them for spiritual warfare) or religious prayer books when you speak to Him. Those words are not your words. Say what you mean and mean what you say. Speak from the heart. Let your yes be yes and your no be no. Keep it simple, honest and direct.

ANYTIME ANYWHERE.
We can talk to Him any place, any time. His spirit dwells within us. If you have a problem or a crisis don't wait. Talk to Him straight away. He is there for you 24/7 for neither Yahuah or Yahusha sleep nor slumber.

DON'T BABBLE LIKE THE PAGANS.
We are told not to babble like pagans. Get to the point. Make your petition known. Say what you came to say. Ask for what you want in His name. Be specific. Shorter prayers are often sharper and more powerful than long drawn-out ones.

ONE ARROW AT A TIME.

An archer loads one arrow in the bow at a time knowing it will find its mark. When talking to Yahuah, make one request at a time. Tell Him what you want. Be specific.

Do not read out an endless wish list. Ask for one thing and focus on it. Believe you have been heard. Know that your petition has been received and its fulfilment is on its way. Imagine it having been delivered. See it as having happened. Imagine life with the prayer answered. Expect things to be resolved, stop worrying, be alert and have faith the blessing is coming.

BE REALISTIC.

Do not ask for ridiculous things like world peace, the end of all wars, the end of all sickness and disease, no more natural disasters or the end of world famine. The entire history of mankind has been given to us already, in advance, in the Dead Sea Scrolls. There is no point in praying for the opposite of what the Creator has told is going to happen. That is not realistic.

BE SPECIFIC.

Be specific about what you want. If you want to be healed from cancer, get to the point and say so. If you want a marital relationship restored, say so. If you need money to pay debts, don't sidestep the issue, just say so. If you want a wayward child to change their ways, say so. If you are unhappy in your career, say so. Be specific and get to the point because He knows what you are going to ask before you do. When you ask for something specific it is easier for it to be answered.

BE PRACTICAL.

Pray for things you want, things that make a difference in your life. Be practical. Pray for physical, mental and spiritual health. Pray for others who belong to Yahuah Elohim. Pray to overcome poverty and misfortune, to overcome infertility and chronic illness, and pray for justice, forgiveness, and a way forward if things are tough. Pray for what you need. Pray for what matters.

DON'T REPEAT YOURSELF.:
Yahuah is not deaf nor forgetful. Constantly repeating our prayer does not make it bigger or louder but suggests a lack of faith. Speak plainly, get to the point and know you have been heard.

GIVE THANKS REPEATEDLY.
Repeating a prayer undermines that prayer. Repeating our thanks empowers it. Focus on expectation. Imagine how much better life will be when your prayer is answered. Dwell on gratitude which is positive energy. Positive energy propels the blessings in our direction. Expect the unexpected. Yahuah Elohim has a wonderful sense of humour. Be open to surprises. Prayers are often answered in the most unexpected ways. Prepare to be amazed!

GETTING TOGETHER.
There is spiritual power when two or more are gathered in prayer, in one accord, focussing on one request such as the healing of a brother or sister in Yahuah from a terminal disease. Praying together is spiritual dynamite.

If a child is sick, or a teenager is going off the rails, or a marriage is falling apart, or the loss of a job, or a home, or the ability to go on, we can turn to Yahuah Elohim as a small group, in powerful prayer. He hears us, always! Prayer with others is immensely powerful. He says, when two or more are gathered in my name, there I will be also.

PREPARE TO BE TESTED.
Get ready to be put to the test. Big blessings, like the healing of a terminal illness, require a lot of positive energy. Being tested to keep the law under difficult circumstances generates even more positive energy. When praying for big things, expect big tests. That is how blessings are unlocked, empowered and delivered.

HOME LIBRARY
FOR SPIRITUAL HEALTH

For those looking to deepen their understanding of the spiritual realm, may I suggest the follow books as a foundation for a home library.

FIRST RECOMMENDATION:
THE BOOK OF JUBILEES

Fig. 23

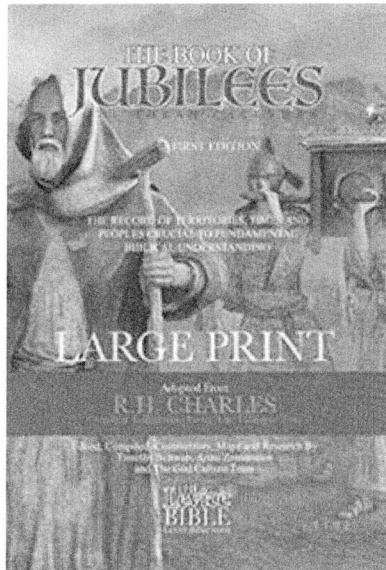

THE BOOK OF JUBILEES

Written by Moses and the Angel of the Presence over three and half thousand years ago, Jubilees is an ideal first purchase for your home library into spiritual health. Jubilees exposes the mystery of demons behind mental illness for what and who they are.

Jubilees teaches spiritual warfare, showing us how we can fight back against the powers of darkness that bring poverty and misfortune. It is essential to understanding the spiritual realm. Our preferred edition is published by the God Culture, an independent group of researchers not affiliated to any religion. Available on Amazon.

SECOND RECOMMENDATION:
THE BOOK OF ENOCH

Fig. 24

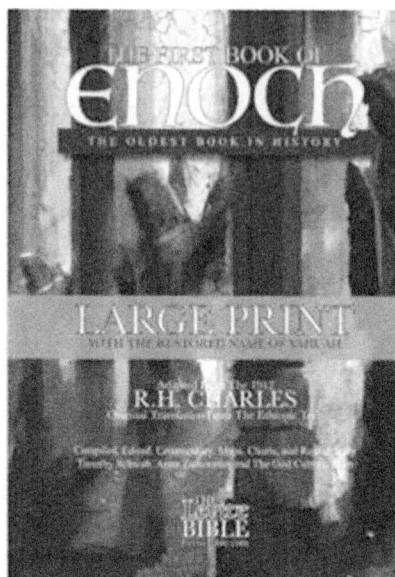

THE BOOK OF ENOCH

Purported to be the oldest book ever written, co-authored by Enoch and the Angel of the Presence. It is a first-hand eye-witness account of life on earth before the great flood in the days of Noah. It documents the falling of the Watcher angels, their procreation with human women and their strange unnatural offspring, the hybrid human giants known as the Nephilim.

Enoch was once part of the Bible until the Roman Catholic Church removed it in the 1600s. It is time to restore it and discover the secrets of the spiritual realm, the mystery of death, eternal life, angelic entities, demons and the Creator.

It is an essential read for those wanting to grow in spiritual health and power. As with Jubilees it is published by the God Culture, a non-religious group of researchers, and is available on Amazon.

Fig. 25

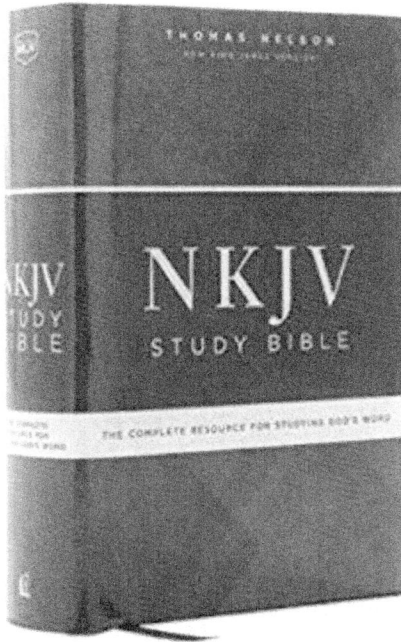

THE 'NEW KING JAMES' STUDY BIBLE

This edition is the most reputable translation among the many English translations available. 'Study' Bibles have extensive explanatory notes to help gain a deeper understanding and are ideal for those starting out on their journey into spiritual health.

Standard King James Bibles do not have additional explanatory notes so are smaller and less costly. There are many formats available on Amazon. There are many second-hand Bibles in good condition at affordable prices too.

Dip in and out of the Bible as often as you are led by the spirit. It is an endless spiritual resource, and a compass on our journey through life.

FOURTH RECOMMENDATION:
STONGS CONCORDANCE

Fig.26

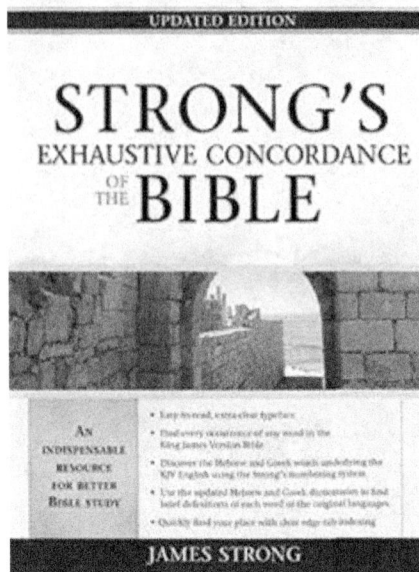

STRONG'S CONCORDANCE

Strong's Concordance is an index of the original Hebrew words used in writing the Old Testament and the Greek words used in writing the New Testament. It is an incredible resource for those wishing to take their understanding of the spiritual realm to a deeper level.

Discover the exact Hebrew words written in the original scrolls, how to write them, say them and what they mean. With a concordance we can verify everything and not be deceived or misled.

Strong's Concordance is widely available online, both new and second hand.

Fig. 27

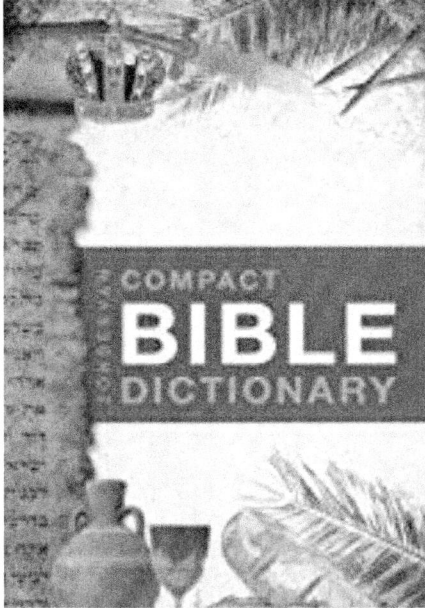

ZONDERVAN BIBLE DICTIONARY

Many Biblical words refer to things we no longer use or have knowledge of today. The Zondervan Bible dictionary has over 5000 entries defining what and who those things, places, and people are.

This bring understanding to texts that would otherwise be difficult to fathom. A very useful resource and available online.

CHAPTER 8

ART TO CALM THE MIND AND STILL THE SPIRIT

ART TO CALM THE MIND
AND STILL THE SPIRIT

Art can calm the mind, still the spirit. It can unlock the imagination which is a powerful fruit of the spirit. These works of art can lead your thoughts into positive territory, helping you to heal.

Full-colour print available from, www.rosaleetuffney.com

Fig.28

GETHSEMANE

Yahusha ha Mashiach cried out in deep distress knowing what lay before Him. It is written that He was comforted during this torment by an angel.

Reflected behind the angel is a suggestion of a cross, foretelling what was to come. The spiritually healthy have the wisdom to know they also have angels appointed to comfort them in moments of fear and distress.

Fig.29

JOURNEY'S END

Everything has a season. Nothing lasts forever. If you have battled a long season of mental illness, or sickness, know that it will not last forever.

Your best life is still ahead. Now it is time to focus on your destiny for your journey still has a long way to go.

Full-colour print available: www.rosaleetuffney.com

Fig. 30.

MONACH OF THE MOOR

Creation is amazing! If Yahuah Elohim can create all this, how easy is it for His spirit to heal us. He tells us not to be anxious about anything, but in every situation, turn to Him. Don't let yesterday take up too much of today.

Full-colour print available at: www.rosaleetuffney.com

Fig. 31

CREATION: DAY 3

Yahusha ha Mashiach said, "let the land produce vegetation, seed bearing plants and trees that bear fruit with seeds in it."

Full-colour print available from www.rosaleetuffney.com

Fig. 32

THE ARK IN STILLNESS

The flood in the days of Noah came to rid the earth of the fallen angels, the Nephilim giants and the corruption of the human DNA. For those who know the origin of the demons behind mental illness, the flood in the days of Noah has particular significance.

Full-colour print available from www.rosaleetuffney.com

Fig. 33

MOTHERHOOD

Our strongest spiritual bond we can have on earth, aside from that with our Creator, is with our parents and our children. When these relationships get broken so does our spirit. Honouring our parents and guiding our children brings a comforting balm to the spirit.

Full-colour print available from www.rosaleetuffney.com

ILLUSTRATIONS

ILLUSTRATIONS

NOTES:

NOTES:

THE END

Printed in Great Britain
by Amazon